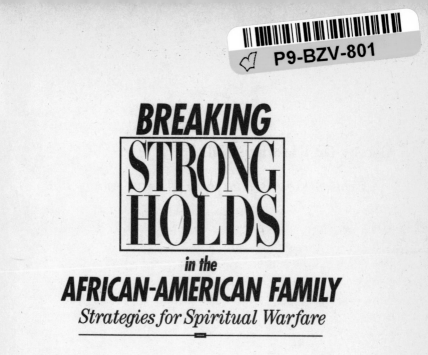

BREAKING STRONG HOLDS

in the
AFRICAN-AMERICAN FAMILY

Strategies for Spiritual Warfare

Also by Dr. Clarence Walker

Biblical Counseling with African-Americans

BREAKING STRONGHOLDS

in the
AFRICAN-AMERICAN FAMILY
Strategies for Spiritual Warfare

Dr. Clarence Walker

ZondervanPublishingHouse
Grand Rapids, Michigan

A Division of HarperCollinsPublishers

Breaking Strongholds in the African-American Family
Copyright © 1996 by Clarence Walker

Requests for information should be addressed to:

⚑ZondervanPublishingHouse
Grand Rapids, Michigan 49530

Library of Congress Cataloging-in-Publication Data

Walker, Clarence Earl.
    Breaking strongholds in the African-American family : strategies for spiritual
warfare / Clarence Walker.
        p. cm.
    ISBN: 0–310–20007–5
    1. Church work with Afro-American families. 2. Afro-American families—
Religious life. 3. Spiritual warfare. I. Title.
BV4526.2.W25   1995
248.4'089'96073–dc20   95–25258
                                                                      CIP

Unless otherwise indicated, Scripture quotations are from the King James Version
of the Bible. Quotations identified as NIV® are from the *Holy Bible: New
International Version* copyright © 1973, 1978, 1984 by the International Bible
Society.

Edited by Victoria L. Johnson
Interior design by Joe Vriend

Printed in the United States of America

---

    96 97 98 99 00 01 02 /❖ DH/ 10 9 8 7 6 5 4 3

To my lovely wife, Ja'Ola, and our sons,
Justin and Arthur, without whose support
this book would not have been written.

Contents

Introduction

The African-American family and its problems have been the focus of national attention for more than four decades. Various social scientists and mental health specialists, both black and white, have proposed a host of theories and reasons for the problems and challenges of the African-American family: (1) The general consensus is that they are victims of racism; (2) the socioeconomic theory suggests that there is a relationship between national economics and the plight of poor black families; (3) the matriarchal legacy theory points to the absence of African-American fathers, creating a large group of female-headed, single-parent homes; (4) the Afroism theory implies that the African-American family's kinship structure and culture are in conflict with the dominant Eurocentric Anglo-Saxon values in our present society. These theories have been put forth at some time or another as the chief explanation for the dysfunction in African-American families.

A host of strategies has been suggested by an assortment of political, economic, religious, and social organizations, both public and private, on how to address these family issues. The problem with most of these theories is the way in which they view human beings. They see man as a creature with a mind and a body, the highest development of the animal kingdom, and the most evolved in the Darwinian evolutionary process. Whatever one's view of mankind will determine the strategy used to solve man's difficulties.

It is my contention that all of these theories have merit and all of them, to one degree or another, explain the problems of the African-American family. However, they do not go far enough, nor adequately explain why the challenges in African-American families exist. I propose another perspective, a biblical view. This understanding begins with the notion that man is created in the image of God (Genesis 1:27–28), that he has a sin nature, that he is totally depraved; and that he is in need of the divine help of God through salvation because he cannot save himself. Furthermore, man has a spiritual enemy named Satan, whose agenda is to destroy God's creation (mankind) and to pervert every relationship and institution concerning man (John 10:10).

My perspective is based upon personal experience as an African-American man who grew up in a difficult family situation and my interaction with other African-Americans who also came from difficult families. I am a marriage and family therapist counseling African-American families. I have studied their predicaments and the Word of God, both academically and personally. This book is a culmination of my experiences and study. My goal is not to point out the African-American family as an evil, negative institution. Nor is it my objective to let my white brothers and sisters off the hook regarding the issue of racism, especially as it is being shown in the ranks of protestant evangelism. The intention of this book is to explain the trouble of African-American family phenomenon in a spiritual way. After putting all of my experiences together and looking at the inadequacy of other theories, I have concluded that many of the problems related to the African-American family dysfunction are the result of spiritual strongholds.

Dr. Clarence Walker

PART ONE

The Strongholds in African-American Families

CHAPTER ONE

What Is a Stronghold?

A stronghold is a forceful stubborn argument, rationale, opinion, idea, and/or philosophy that is formed and resistant to the knowledge of Jesus Christ. The skillful use of spiritual weapons in spiritual warfare is required to break a stronghold.

> *For though we walk in the flesh, we do not war after the flesh: (For the weapons of our warfare are not carnal* [weapons of flesh and blood], *but mighty through God to the pulling down* [overthrow and destruction] *of strong holds;) Casting down imaginations, and every high thing that exalteth itself against the knowledge of God, and bringing into captivity every thought to the obedience of Christ (2 Corinthians 10:3–5).*

Let's look closer at verse 5 from the Amplified Bible.

> *[Inasmuch as we] refute arguments and theories and reasonings and every proud and lofty thing that sets itself up against the (true) knowledge of God; and we lead every thought and purpose away captive unto the obedience of Christ, the Messiah, the Anointed One.*

In this passage of Scripture, first of all, there exists a form of spiritual bondage known as a stronghold. The Greek word for stronghold is *ochuroma*. It means "to fortify through the idea of holding something safely." A stronghold is like a castle, fortress, or it can be a stubborn argument. Secondly, the arguments, reasonings, opinions, ideologies, philosophies, and rationales are contrary or diametrically opposed to the knowledge of Christ, therefore they are satanic. Anything that opposes Christ is from His enemy, the devil, thus strongholds are from Satan and his demonic host. Thirdly, strongholds are so resilient that they require weapons in order to combat them. They are not things you can talk down or negotiate with. They don't go away with time. Spiritual strongholds will not be complained away, regulated, or picketed down. They do not self-destruct. They must be destroyed, brought down, obliterated, and demolished. One must wage warfare when dealing with strongholds. An individual must have both a soldier's attitude and a soldier's arms in order to overcome them.

DESCRIPTION

Strongholds Are Resistant to Change.

You know you are dealing with a stronghold when

- A family member refuses to alter their behavior even though they know it will be of personal benefit
- Marital and/or family problems have not changed over a period of time, and have even gotten worse, despite all human effort
- Marriage partners or other family members are blind to their own faults, but are able to see everyone else's
- Family members cannot control human desires and impulses and have no desire to do so
- A family member is consistently and openly hostile to the Christian faith

Strongholds Are Restrictive.

Strongholds are like an enclosure that is fortified with thick and high stone walls, similar to the walls in Middle Eastern cities that are described as being 15 feet thick and 25 feet high.[1]

When a person is bound in a stronghold, they find protection and security in that stronghold. One of the reasons why people will not give up their behavior, idea, philosophy, or opinion, even when it is contrary to God's Word, is because they find certain feelings of safety, security, and familiarity in them. The Canaanites of Jericho did not know that the very walls they thought would protect them would become their destruction. "Now Jericho was straitly shut up because of the children of Israel: none went out, and none came in" (Joshua 6:1).

None went out and none came in. When someone is bound by a stronghold, they will let nothing in and nothing out. You can give them truth all day long; you can show them love, kindness, and compassion; you can give them warnings, admonitions, exhortations, or threats, yet they won't let it in. They are well defended. Their walls are up. They are committed to self-protection and defense toward all they deem as invaders or intruders. They are either actively or passively resistant. They can be hostile or cordial in their defenses, but be well assured that they are "shut up" to the truth, to deliverance, to help, and even to impending judgment. Thus, anyone who threatens the safety of their stronghold is the enemy, and they will fend off all who come to challenge their spiritual and psychological status quo. Anything, no matter how truthful, that does not line up with their perverted view is to be resisted at all costs. "A brother offended is harder to be won than a strong city: and their contentions are like the bars of a castle [fortress or stronghold]" (Proverbs 18:19).

Strongholds Are Ruled by Authoritative Principalities.

Every stronghold has a king ruler governing the forces and reigning over the stronghold. The stronghold itself and the king of the stronghold are distinguished from each other. The stronghold must be destroyed, and the king must be defeated as well. If the stronghold is brought down but the king is not brought down, then the ruler will simply relocate, rebuild, and continue his reign.

When Joshua conquered Canaan to move the Israelites into the Promised Land, he had to overcome thirty-one cities. He not only had to demolish the city, but also defeat their kings. "And thou shalt do to Ai and her king as thou didst unto Jericho and her king" (Joshua 8:2).

Notice how the Word of God distinguished the king and the stronghold from one another. Joshua had to wage war against and overcome natural rulers.

We on the other hand have to wage war and defeat spiritual rulers, "For we wrestle not against flesh and blood, but against principalities, against powers, against the rulers of the darkness of this world, against spiritual wickedness in high places" (Ephesians 6:12).

Paul identified the king rulers of the spiritual Jerichos and Ais; for, unlike Joshua, our enemy is not natural, carnal, or human. This is an important factor for us to understand, because Christians are notorious for fighting human enemies and failing to see that oftentimes the people whom we fight are simply carrying out the orders of an invisible ruler who is their lord. Everybody, whether they are aware of it or not, must obey some "lord." Hence, we waste so much time, energy, and effort because we have not learned to identify the real enemy.

Strongholds Are Often Inherited.

When a family, a couple, or a people hold on to opinions, behaviors, ideas, and arguments that are contrary to the Word of God, they become the enemy of God, and, therefore, hate God. The Bible says to love Him is to keep His commandments. The result is that strongholds can be passed down from one family generation to another as a legacy, "... visiting the iniquity of the fathers upon the children unto the third and fourth generation of them that hate me" (Exodus 20:5b). "As is the mother, so is her daughter" (Ezekiel 16:44). For example, in Jericho Canaanite grandparents, parents, and children were inside the Jericho wall forming three and four generations of people of the same blood lineage living together inside of Jericho. In the same way, we see three and four generations of African-American families who have the same stronghold, passing it from one generation to the next. As a family therapist, I am very aware of the multigenerational nature of African-Americans' dysfunctions. I have counseled families in which clients were experiencing codependence, marriage conflicts, substance abuse, third- and fourth-generation patterns of divorce, and abuse.

Strongholds Are Defensive.

They usually have an army of soldiers, armed and perched on the walls, ready to defend them. The Bible reminds us that Satan uses fiery darts (Ephesians 6:16). These darts represent three different types of projectiles which can be fiery stones, fiery arrows, and fiery javelins. The fact that all three are fiery indicates that these soldiers are serious about protecting the stronghold. They mean business. They will try to maim, kill, and destroy anyone who tries to take their fortress.

CHAPTER TWO

Types of Strongholds

Strongholds differ from family to family. They are built on various foundations.

FEAR

The first foundation of a stronghold is fear. Fear can masquerade as hostility or aggressiveness. When King Saul threw a javelin at David, fear was at the root of the aggressive act. Often, when I have seen hostile defensive African-American clients, I have discerned that their hostility is a cover-up for their fear. This challenging stronghold in African-American family relationships can manifest itself as a fear of closeness or intimacy, causing the husband to distance himself from his wife, or vice versa. This distancing behavior can result in an extramarital affair as the ultimate way to avoid closeness. This person who pulls away may have been sexually abused or may be following a family history of avoiding intimacy. Some families are not close to each other, and that becomes their legacy. Sometimes people who have lost loved ones to tragedy experience a pain so great that they vow never to get close to anyone again. Therefore, they avoid the pain of another person leaving or dying.

For a woman who has been sexually abused as a child, sex and intimacy may be difficult things for her to adjust to because she associates them with abuse. Since abuse is a form of control, the victim usually fears being controlled by men and sees sex as a means of such control. The fear of rejection or abandonment may create a clingy, dependent, codependent, and possessive individual, who is always looking to her spouse to give her the love and attention she never received from her family growing up.

The fear of being hurt may cause family members to be defensive and self-protective and intolerant of criticism or correction. As long as fear is present, a person cannot give mature love and often cannot receive mature love. "He that feareth is not made perfect [mature] in love" (1 John 4:18).

The fear of being wrong has caused many an African-American man to hold on to a position or make a decision that was destructive to himself or his family. The fear of being alone has caused many an African-American mother to hold on to her children, interfering with their lives and violating boundaries even into her children's adult years, thus gaining her the title of the "meddling-in-law."

ANGER

A second foundation of strongholds is anger. Much of the violence evident in the African-American community is a manifestation of this stronghold. Today's African-American youth are the most violent generation we have ever seen. Many of these youths are angry at everyone. They are upset with fathers who are violent, neglectful, or absent. They are mad at mothers who have to play both the mother and father role. They are hostile toward the white power structure that continues to oppress them. African-Americans are an angry people. Sometimes this anger is mistakenly interpreted by whites as

African-American racism. For the most part, African-American people are not racist (racism being defined as racial prejudice coupled with the economic, political, and social power to enforce it), however, they carry a lot of rage inside.

As one who has worked on the streets of Philadelphia with a Black Muslim gang, and as a community leader in Southwest Philadelphia side by side with Muslims, I have discovered that Black Muslims are very angry with white America. Two African-American psychiatrists, Price M. Cobbs and William Grier, were the first to designate this hostility as "black rage."[1] This is a good description of the anger many African-Americans feel. When "black rage" is vented in the home it results in the physical abuse of the spouse and children. When it is released in the community, it sometimes can take the form of violent crimes, gang conflicts, murder, assault, and vandalism. When it is expressed in music, it comes out in the negative rap music of such artists as "Two Live Crew," "Ice T," and others. When it comes out in sociopolitical arenas, it produces movements such as the Black Panthers of the sixties and some of the more radical Afrocentric groups of the nineties. When anger is manifested in religion, it takes on the form of the Nation of Islam and other Muslim groups. There is a consistent, seething rage burning in many African-American people.

The dictionary defines rage as, "an overmastering passion of any kind; to behave with passion, especially with furious, violent, uncontrollable anger; a fit of violent wrath; an intense feeling, or passion."[2] The Bible teaches that we are to put off all of these, anger, wrath, and malice (Colossians 3:8). The original Greek word for anger is *orge*, which means a violent passion; anger as a state of mind, impulse, or desire. The word "wrath" in the original Greek means "to move impetuously; a violent motion or passion of the mind; an outburst of wrath from inward indignation."[3] There is a difference between anger (*orge*) and wrath (*thumos*).

Thumos indicates a more agitated condition of the mind, frequently with the view of taking revenge. *Orge* is less sudden in rise than *thumos*, but more lasting in nature. *Thumos* is more of an inward feeling and *orge* more of an active emotion. *Thumos* may issue in revenge, though it doesn't necessarily include it. It is characteristic that it quickly blazes up and quickly subsides, though that is not necessarily implied in each case.[4]

Many African-Americans live in the stronghold of *orge*. It becomes their ultimate and constant defense, an emotional fortification against a racist society they have learned not to trust. But when they perceive an attack, *thumos* (wrath) becomes their offense. *Orge* are the walls of Jericho and *thumos* are the archer's arrows shot from the wall.

IDOLATRY

Occultism

Besides fear and anger, a third stronghold foundation in the African-American family is idolatry, expressed in the form of the occult. African-Americans came from a polytheistic[5] African culture where often the most powerful person was the witch doctor, the charmer, or the magician, not the tribal chief or national king.[6] This fascination and involvement with the occult was not destroyed during slavery. This practice survived, especially in the South. Root workers, as they are called, can cast a spell or provide a charm which claims to remove curses, heal bodies, and change bad luck into good. Some charmers believe they have genuine power and use it to help or control others, while some are phonies who exploit the misfortunes of others and capitalize on their fears, which are deeply rooted in superstitions. Older African-Americans still will resort to these root workers, and many will occasionally journey back to the South to consult the family charmer.[7]

For today's Buppies (Black Yuppies), the practice of the occult takes more modern forms, such as a preoccupation with astrology and horoscopes. Many African-Americans are into black magic, sorcery, and contemporary witchcraft. Some professionals and well-educated African-Americans have turned to Egyptology, sun worship, or Mother Goddess worship (of Asherah or Isis) as an alternative to a white male image of Christianity.[8] One of the native meanings of the name Africa is land of the "spirit people." Unfortunately, this is truly the case.

Most African-American bookstores stock shelves of books directly or indirectly related to the African-American sorcery, Egyptology, spiritism, astrology, magic, and occult. In many communities occult shops and businesses still exist and many of them have been in operation for years even when other entrepreneurial African-American efforts have failed. I can recall a few years ago being in a bookstore looking for an African-American history book when a young African-American female about twelve years old walked up to the counter and calmly asked a store worker if they carried the "Devil's Bible." They didn't. A few of the adults in the store looked at each other, and our eyes said it all. We were shocked at how someone so young was already interested in reading about the occult.

Furthermore, several African-Americans are part of secret fraternal orders such as the Masons, Eastern Star, and the Elks. When such people hold positions in the church, they can be a powerful force to reckon with. These orders are often cultish (devoted to a person, idea, or thing; a group united by allegiances to a movement or figure), if not occultism (a secret or mysterious practice or belief influenced by supernatural powers). God told his people:

> When you enter the land the LORD your God is giving you, do not learn to imitate the detestable ways of the nations there. Let no one be found among you who sacrifices his son or daughter in the fire, who practices divination or sorcery, interprets omens, engages in witchcraft, or cast spells, or

who is a medium or spiritist or who consults the dead. Anyone who does these things is detestable to the LORD, and because of these detestable practices the LORD your God will drive out those nations before you (Deuteronomy 18:9–12 NIV).

Witchcraft and Drugs

The apostle Paul lists witchcraft among the works of the flesh (Galatians 5:20). The Greek word is *pharmakeia*, from which we devise the word "pharmacy"—a word associated with drugs and medication, both curative and poisonous. Moreover, *pharmakeia* is further interpreted to mean illicit or illegal pharmaceuticals; magical use of drugs and spells; and poisoning, the use of drugs by someone whose purpose it is to inflict injury.

This biblical and historical description of witchcraft and pharmaceuticals describes today's most plaguing social problem, especially in the African-American community: the drug epidemic. We call it a drug problem, but God calls it "witchcraft." Drug pushers are the modern day witches and sorcerers. Where you find drugs, you will find witchcraft, and where you find witchcraft, you will find drugs. That is the reason why the epidemic continues, despite the vigilance of the United States and other nations to reduce drug use and to stop drug traffic. African-American people do not have a monopoly on the drug problem. There are studies that show that whites, in some cases, have more of a problem. The difference is that for African-Americans, drugs are part of our African religious heritage. You cannot fight witchcraft with law enforcement officers, technology, drug agents, and guns, because they are carnal and witchcraft is spiritual. Campaign slogans such as "Just Say No" are a joke. How can someone just say no to a witch? How does one resist the temptation of a sorcerer?

African-Americans have a cultural predisposition to drugs because they are so much a part of our African heritage. Witch doctors and charmers frequently gave people special potions and medications. When God told Israel to avoid the witchcraft and sorcery of other nations, He was primarily talking about those nations who were descendants of Ham, namely the Canaanites and the Kamite Africans of Egypt (Exodus 7:11, 22). These nations did not repent of their sorceries (Revelation 9:2). The word "sorceries" here is also the Greek word *pharmakiah*. We could say this verse another way, that they did not repent of their illicit drugs and enhancement spells.

African-Americans are descendants of Ham, via his son Cush, whose name means black, dark-skinned, or ebony-colored. The Hamite peoples' religious practices often included the use of drugs, spells, and enchantments. African-American drug addicts are often simply continuing the legacy of their ancestors. The effects of drugs on users can appropriately be described by words such as enchantment, trance, and spell. We will never solve the drug problem until we stop calling it drugs and start calling it what God calls it—witchcraft; the crisis will not be eliminated until we stop seeing it as a social issue and start viewing it as a spiritual issue; and we must stop relying on carnal weapons to defeat it and start relying on spiritual weapons. (We will deal at length with our arsenal of spiritual weapons later in the book.) This is just one aspect of idolatry in the African-American community.

Worshiping People

A second form of idolatry is that African-American people sometimes worship and idolize their sport celebrities, entertainers, politicians, and yes, even preachers to the point of making them gods. This helps to create a situation in which many of our high profile African-American men develop a "Nimrod" complex. (We will return to this subject a little later when we look at spiritual strongholds in the African-American male.) The result is we create men with god complexes like Father Divine and Sweet Daddy Grace. The majority of the people who died in Guyana with Jim Jones were minorities. Here again, this trend toward making our leaders gods is rooted in our African heritage. In Africa, the kings were oftentimes considered to be gods. The pharaohs of the Kamite Africans of Egypt and many African kings as well as queens were considered to be deities. This "Afroism" (a tradition, interest, or ideal from Africa) has been maintained from our past and has become a stronghold to us as a people. God warned Israel consistently about idolatry:

> *Thou shalt have no other gods before me. Thou shalt not make unto thee any graven image, or any likeness of any thing that is in heaven above, or that is in the earth beneath, or that is in the water under the earth: Thou shalt not bow thyself down to them, nor serve them; for I the LORD thy God am a jealous God, visiting the iniquity of the fathers upon the children unto the third and fourth generation of them that hate me (Exodus 20:3–5).*

This passage is clear. When a people turn to idolatry and don't serve the true God, the negative consequences can last three to four generations.

CHAPTER THREE

Strongholds Imprisoning African-American Males

There are spiritual strongholds that specifically relate to African-American men.

THE FEAR OF INTIMACY SYNDROME

Many of the African-American women whom we see in therapy complain about the black male's lack of affection and attention. They often say how white men are more affectionate and attentive. One could argue the accuracy of this perception, but the point is that the belief that African-American men are not affectionate is widely held among the sisters. As an African-American male and a therapist who counsels men, it is my judgment that this perception is valid. We need to look at the root of this lack of affection in African-American males. It is derived from a stronghold of fear, namely the fear of intimacy.

Fatherless Homes

First, Satan has hatched an effective plan to destroy African-American marriages because he fears united black couples and what they can do for the kingdom of God together. The enemy sets up the African-American male to fail as a husband in this area, and the plot starts early as we grow up in our families. Many men grow up in fatherless homes and (this writer included) do not know who or even where their fathers are. They often are raised in homes where they feel rejected, neglected, and abandoned by their fathers. Experiencing rejection himself damages a man's ability to be close to someone.

Poor Examples

Even when African-American fathers are present, they are not usually affectionate men. They distance themselves from their wives and children. As a result, a young African-American male coming up in such an environment witnesses and watches his father's physical distance from his mother. African-American fathers often get high marks for being hard workers and providers, but low marks in the area of affection with spouse and children. Many African-American men follow the distancing legacy; the "don't get too close" pattern of their fathers.

Fear of Loss

African-American men tend to have shorter life spans than white men by virtue of their higher susceptibility to cancer, diabetes, high blood pressure, stroke, AIDS, or the tragedy of murder in a highly violent, hostile environment. Moreover sizable numbers of African-American men are more likely to work in blue-collar jobs, which often involve hazardous conditions and exposure to deadly toxins. Since an African-American male child may see his father taken away from him early in life, the possible result may be that he avoids getting close to anyone he loves for fear that they may tragically be taken away from him also. In this situation, a fear of closeness and intimacy is born.

Too Much Responsibility

The fourth factor related to this problem is that if the father is absent or deceased, all too frequently the young African-American male child, usually the oldest (but not in every case), has to become the man of the house, growing up too soon, and becoming a "parentified" child (a child taking on a parent's responsibility). Such a young male will develop a close attachment to his mother, as he is now the emotional substitute for his father. He develops strong loyalties to his mother that continue even if he gets married. The problem is that he remains emotionally loyal to his mother and becomes afraid of getting too close to his wife for fear of being disloyal to the mother. Therefore, he may be distant from the wife in order to remain close to the mother. The Bible says, "[For this cause] shall a man leave his father and his mother, and shall cleave unto his wife: and they shall be one flesh" (Genesis 2:24).

A man is unable to cleave to his wife if he has not emotionally and physically left his parent(s). This obviously becomes a frustrating situation to the wife, and these kinds of relationships often end in painful divorce. So Satan sets this strategy early in the African-American family, knowing that it will have a domino effect from parent to child. The seeds of future marital discord are sown early in this manner.

Fear of Rejection

The same type of family occurrences mentioned which leads to the fear of intimacy can lead to another kind of fear: the fear of rejection. African-American men can be very sensitive and defensive toward the slightest hint of disapproval. They will generally respond with either fight (in the form of violence or physical confrontation) or flight (they run away from and abandon their families). Fear has been one of Satan's greatest strategies in keeping African-American men bound in a stronghold.

THE BLOODY WARRIOR SYNDROME

This second stronghold in African-American men has anger as its foundation. Black people are not more violent than other races—contrary to popular opinion. In fact, if one looks at European history with the rapings, pillaging [destruction] and violence of the so-called Crusades; the heinous crimes against Jews by the German Nazis; and the horrible torturing tactics of the Romans, one could argue that, historically, Europeans are more notorious in the arena of violence. Nevertheless, African-Americans experience their share of violence, both as a present reality as well as their African heritage. Few would argue with the fact that African-Americans tend to have higher rates of violence and homicide, as evidenced by the fact that the leading cause of death among African-American males ages 15–34 is homicide.[1] Some of this propensity for violence can be explained by the fact that African-American men are "warriors" by nature. You will find no greater warrior, no more valiant a soldier, no more skillful a fighter than among black men. It is for this reason that they excel in competitive sports, especially boxing, basketball, and football.

Even the Bible acknowledges the warrior nature of black men. The first man in the Bible to become a great warrior and champion was a black man named Nimrod.

> *Cush was the father of Nimrod, who grew to be a mighty warrior on the earth. He was a mighty hunter before the LORD; That is why it is said, "Like Nimrod a mighty hunter before the LORD" (Genesis 10:8–9 NIV).*

The name Cush means black or black-skinned. The Cushites settled in Africa and Asia.[2] The name "Ethiopia" comes from the Greek name for Cush. The Cushites were a tall, smooth-skinned people. They were feared far and wide, an aggressive nation of strange speech (Isaiah 18:1 NIV).

The Bible says Nimrod was the son of Cush. So a black man, one of the patriarchs of the African peoples became the first great warrior in the Bible. He is referred to as a "mighty" warrior. The word *mighty* in the Hebrew is *gibbor*, which means champion, conqueror, giant, a great warrior, and super-hero. Legends concerning Nimrod claim he fought and defeated animals with his bare hands. Even Satan fears the warrior nature of black men.

THE NIMROD SYNDROME

However, Nimrod's notoriety extends beyond his warrior prowess. Nimrod had a problem that symbolizes the third stronghold often evident in African-American men, namely "pride." He believed his own press. Nimrod became overly impressed with his own achievements. He defied himself based on his incomparable accomplishments. He developed a level of pride that made him feel he was a god. Nimrod thought he could do anything, anywhere, anytime. The man simply fell in love with himself. His pride got the best of him.

Under Nimrod's leadership, the whole population of the earth believed they could build a tower to heaven. They said, "Come, let us build ourselves a city, with a tower that reaches to the heavens, so that we may make a name for ourselves" (Genesis 11:4 NIV).

I believe the statement "make a name for ourselves" alludes to that spirit of Nimrod transferred to the people of the earth. This Cushite champion truly made a name for himself. He was highly regarded and well known. "He was a mighty hunter before the LORD" (Genesis 10:8 NIV).

The word "name" in the original language is *shem* or *sem*, which means a memorial of individuality, fame, authority, renown, mark, memory, and reputation. In other words, Nimrod encouraged the people to become famous, renowned, and leave their mark. He wanted them to take steps to make sure that they would always be in the history books and that their reputation endured.

Wanting to be remembered is not a bad thing; it is what we want to be remembered for that can be bad or good. It is okay to be remembered for one's integrity, generosity, or charity. But Nimrod and this ancient populace wanted "to make a name for ourselves." "Let us build ourselves a city with a tower that reached to the heavens."

The word "city" is *ayar*, a fortified place with watch towers, a camp, a *stronghold*. The word "tower" is *migdalah*, meaning a lofty platform or rostrum, a watch tower, a castle, a small fortress, a podium, a pulpit. It is believed by some scholars that this tower was a ziggurat, a pyramid-like temple structure.[3] The ziggurats were massive terraced towers built by Mesopotamian peoples as temples to their principle gods.[4] The word "heaven" in the original language is *shumeh* or *samayim*, meaning to be lofty, aloft, the firmament. The word can mean sky or realm of sky—sun and moon—or dwelling place of God.[5] Therefore, Nimrod and those he led wanted to build a stronghold, a fortified city, and, within it, a ziggurat-like temple of worship so high that its top would reach into heaven, through the firmament, extending to the stars and even reaching the abode of God.

The problem is, this Nimrod attitude is displayed by many black men when they achieve fame. And so often, because we lack positive role models in the African-American community, we tend to take the few famous men that we have and make Nimrods (human gods) out of them. It doesn't matter whether it is Michael Jackson with the music of his mouth or Michael Jordan with the music of his moves; if it is O. J. or Dr. J, a Martin Luther King or a B. B. King (and there are even a few who worship Don King).

Nimrod built a stronghold of worship, a tower of power with the primal purpose of fame. Babel was a "stronghold of fame." What it became was a source of division and confusion—Babel means confusion. Until African-Americans as a people learn to worship God, every time we build our strongholds of fame they will ultimately end in more division and confusion for us as a people. An oppressor knows how to discourage African-American people who make idols out of men. Therefore, they kill our gods and leave us hopeless.

NEO-POLYGAMOUS SEXUALITY

Polygamy (having more than one mate at one time) and in some cases polyandry (having more than one husband at a time) were commonly accepted in the motherland. Among African-American men this practice is still condoned, which accounts for the high number of extramarital affairs and subsequent breakups of African-American marriages. Extramarital affairs cause sixty percent of African-American marriages to end. Moreover, since there were few options available to African-American men to achieve status in society, they have exercised the privilege of their manliness and attempted to achieve power in the bedroom.[6] Black men are not more sexually immoral than white men. In fact, the heritage of African coital practices was such that the typical ancient African only made love to his wife a certain number of times in his lifetime. Whatever sexual practices African-Americans have may in fact be mere mimicry of the sexual practices of the majority white culture. However, there is one practice that we have maintained as an Afroism—that is having more than one woman as a sexual partner.

In my counseling practice I often have my clients do genograms (family trees). It is not unusual at all to find that the African-American father has two, or, in some cases, three families. Having half brothers and sisters or unknown brothers and sisters is a common phenomenon for African-American people. At present, more than one out of every two children born in the African-American community are born out of wedlock. Too many African-American men are making babies that they can't care for and don't care about. Thus we have a situation in which Afroistic cultural dynamics are in conflict with biblical teachings. My response is, "Let God be true, but every man a liar" (Romans 3:4).

This polygamous heritage of ours has created an impoverished group of African-American children who often live in female-headed, single-parent homes or children who witness divided African-American marriages. It is a formidable stronghold that must come down.

Hence, the fear of intimacy and closeness, the anger of the bloody warrior syndrome, the idolatry of false worship and witchcraft, and the immorality of polygamous sexual practices in African-American men are four of the major strongholds that we must target for spiritual demolition.

CHAPTER FOUR

Strongholds Imprisoning African-American Females

We must not be so focused on the African-American male that we forget about the African-American woman in our discussion of spiritual strongholds in the family.

THE JEZEBEL SYNDROME

One of the most resilient strongholds among African-American women is the Jezebel syndrome. When Jezebel is mentioned, her name is usually associated with a seductive female who is promiscuous. However, a careful study of the biblical account of this woman shows that the bigger issue was her quest for power, control, and the predominance of her religious ideas. Jezebel was a dominant, controlling woman. At the foundation of her quest for control was her pride.

It is my belief that Jezebel was a black woman. She was a Zidonian, the daughter of Ethbaal, the king of the Sidonians and Tyrians (1 Kings 16:31). ("Sidonians" or "Zidonians" is the ancient term for Phoenicians [1 Kings 5:6].) The Sidonians were descendants of Sidon, the first son of Canaan. Canaan was the youngest grandson of Ham, and Ham means warm, dark, hot, and black (Genesis 10:6, 15). Josephus, a Jewish historian, and St. Augustine, an African church father, state that Ham's people occupied Sidon.[1] Dr. Cheikh Anita Diop, a historian, says that the Canaanite Phoenicians (Sidonians) and the Africans of Egypt both have a Cushite origin[2] and that the name "Cush" (as stated earlier) means black-skinned. Pitford says that an image of a Phoenician priestess found in Carthage had Negro features, suggesting she belonged to the African race. Berthelon says these people had very brown skin, and most often their lips were thick and they had prominent cheekbones.[3] J. A. Rogers states that the Phoenicians were Negroes[4] (meaning a people from African descent and Negroid features). Thus, we conclude that Jezebel was a descendant of Ham by way of Canaan, and therefore she was a dark-skinned woman.[5] Jezebel enjoyed being in control. Unfortunately, many African-American women also enjoy being in control and are bound by the Jezebel stronghold. To fully comprehend the Jezebel syndrome, we need to consider its impact in the home as well as in the African-American church.

Jezebel worshiped the religion Baal-Asherah.[6] In Zidonian and Canaanite religion, it was the mother goddess who dominated. Often the mother goddess was depicted in sacred texts as nursing a son. According to the myths and legends, the mother often married the son. Close examination of the marriage of Jezebel and Ahab shows it was more of a mother/son type relationship than that of a husband and wife. Jezebel was the marital mother and Ahab the marital son.

Jezebel was the ultimate head of her house, not Ahab. He followed her lead and reversed God's order for the home. When a Jezebel marries, she often marries an Ahab; dependent, placating, spineless, and weak. She can dominate him. In 1 Timothy 2:12 we read that a woman is not "to usurp." The

Greek word used is *authenteho*, which means to dominate over; to be absolute master; to exercise power and authority over as an aristocrat; to act by one's own authority and power.

God said to Eve concerning her husband Adam, "Thy desire shall be to thy husband, and he shall rule over thee" (Genesis 3:16). Paul says, "The head of every man is Christ, and the head of the woman is the man" (1 Corinthians 11:3).

The Jezebel/mother and Ahab/son marriage arrangement is contrary to these biblical passages. They invert the authority roles, which leads to perverted marital roles.

Of the couples who come to me for marriage counseling, the most common type (to one degree or another) is the mother/son couple type. One of the frequent negative consequences of the mother/son relationship is extramarital affairs. This type of husband will often be unfaithful to his wife because if she plays the role of the controlling mother, he often responds by playing the role of the rebellious son. Furthermore, if a wife acts like a mother, a husband will distance himself from her sexually because he doesn't want to make love to his mother. That is an emotional taboo, and he might go out and find himself another lover!

In terms of her response at home, the Jezebel woman disrespects her husband's authority. Jezebel said to Ahab, "Is this how you act as king over Israel?" (1 Kings 21:7 NIV). Such a statement, even from a queen, is not how one addresses a king. It illustrates the level of disrespect Jezebel had for Ahab. Jezebels give their husbands commands instead of suggestions. "Get up and eat" (1 Kings 21:7 NIV). She didn't say, "Honey, I think you need to have something to eat," which would have been a suggestion; instead, she gave her husband a command. Jezebels possess a take-over spirit that usurps their husbands' authority: "I'll get you the vineyard of Naboth" (1 Kings 21:7 NIV). What she was saying to Ahab was, "You couldn't do it, so I'm taking charge now." She didn't ask for his input, nor did she get his permission.

Finally, Jezebels manipulate situations in the background to make it appear the work of their husband, when in fact they are behind the action. "So she wrote letters in *Ahab's name*, placed his seal on them, and sent them to the elders and nobles who lived in Naboth's city with him" (1 Kings 21:8 NIV, italics mine).

In church, Jezebel types create a lot of havoc. They resent male leadership and will frequently be at odds with a male pastor. They tend to resent the pastor's wife, because Jezebels want to replace her as the most powerful and influential woman in the church. They usually will gravitate to positions of visible leadership and many go into the ministry, especially the pastorate, because they love being called "prophetess." In the book of Revelation Christ admonishes the church of Thyatira concerning their tolerance of a woman there with a Jezebel spirit. He says, "Nevertheless, I have this against you: You tolerate that woman Jezebel, who calls herself a prophetess. By her teaching she misleads my servants into sexual immorality and the eating of food sacrificed to idols" (Revelation 2:20 NIV). You will notice that the Lord says she "calls herself a prophetess" (preacher). This is not to put down the many gifted and anointed women of God who truly are called vessels. Jezebels are a different story. They were never called by God to be prophetesses or preachers. Jezebels are dangerous to the spiritual development of a church if they are in a teaching position, because they will often teach their own doctrinal revelations and will introduce licenses and freedoms that the pastor has preached against.

Moreover, as Revelation 2:20 suggests, there is always some overt or covert sexual immorality associated with Jezebels. She may quietly or openly have lesbian, bisexual, or adulterous tendencies. She may even secretly engage in such activities. It is not unusual for Jezebels to produce homosexual sons or lesbian daughters; in fact, most often their daughters are just like them and carry on their mothers' controlling nature to the next generation. In some cases, the daughters can be worse, as was the case with Jezebel's daughter Athaliah. The daughter was as destructive, and in some cases, more destructive, than the mother (2 Kings 11:1; 2 Chronicles 22:2). Jezebels tend to be religiously seductive and personally charismatic. They are able to attract other women to serve as their flunkies. They often meet secretly, plotting their strategies against their male pastor. Jezebel is very revengeful. When embarrassed, she will plot against someone, as Jezebel did Elijah. "Now Ahab told Jezebel everything Elijah had done and how he had killed all the prophets with the sword. So Jezebel sent a messenger to Elijah to say, 'May the gods deal with me, be it ever so severely, if by this time tomorrow I do not make your life like that of one of them" (1 Kings 19:1–2 NIV).

Jezebel is an unusually vindictive woman and a religious witch in two respects. First, she is rebellious against authority, and the Bible says that rebellion is as the sin of witchcraft (1 Samuel 15:23). Second, many Jezebels resort to actual witchcraft and sorcery to bring down their enemies. Jehu said of Jezebel, "her witchcrafts are so many" (2 Kings 9:22). To face Jezebel is to do battle with a witch.

It is sad but true that many African-American women have inherited the legacy of their Hamitic sister Jezebel and are destroying both their homes and their churches. The Jezebel syndrome thrives best in an environment and among a people who have experienced the diabolical, systematic destruction of their men. They have witnessed the infantilizing and emasculating of their male population.

THE CUTTING TONGUE

A second spiritual stronghold in African-American women is the "cutting tongue." It has been said that no one can lay you out like black woman. Whether one agrees with that statement or not, the negative and painful words that come from the lips of African-American women is challenging indeed. The Scriptures teach that

"Grievous [*hurting*] words stir up anger" (Proverbs 15:1), and "There is that speaketh like the piercings of a sword: but the tongue of the wise is health" (Proverbs 12:18). This biting tongue has been used to destroy the self-esteem of husbands and children. It is often the result of a matriarchal legacy of generations in which daughter, mother, grandmother, and even great-grandmother exhibit the use of the same kind of cutting words. It was the negative cutting words of Delilah, another black woman in the Scriptures, that ultimately brought Samson to his end. Delilah was a Philistine (Judges 16:4–20). Philistines where descendants of Ham's second son, Mizraim (Genesis 10:13–14). Delilah, therefore, was also a Hamite. She was a beautiful, dark-skinned woman, but it was not her beauty that got to Samson. It was her negative words: "With such nagging she prodded him day after day until he was tired to death" (Judges 16:16 NIV). The King James Version says she "pressed" him. The Hebrew word for "press" means to distress, oppress, press upon, or to be an oppressor. Delilah did this until Samson's soul was "vexed," which in Hebrew is *qatsar*, meaning to cut down, discourage, grieve, and cut off. Hence, she oppressed him with her words to the point where he felt cut down, cut off, discouraged, and grieved to death.

CODEPENDENCY

A third stronghold for African-American women is codependency. Daughters of alcoholics and addicts often marry the same type of man and become codependent: they are addicted to the alcoholic or addict. Typically, these women have low self-esteem. They often have a need to be needed, and have a high tolerance for abuse, both physical and verbal. They will put up with a lot of negative behavior from men, in some instances defending and rationalizing the man's behavior. African-American women tend to have an unhealthy emotional bond to men and a great fear of rejection. This type of woman often becomes clingy, possessive, and has a fear of being alone. She also tends to be resistant to any counsel that suggests she leave her man. Co-dependency coupled with low self-esteem is a challenging stronghold to bring down.

THE TAMAR COMPLEX

When an African-American woman has been sexually assaulted, sexually abused, or physically abused, it may lead to a "Tamar Complex." Tamar was raped by her half brother Amnon, which made her a victim of rape and incest. This incident ruined her life; she was never the same afterwards. Samuel says that as a result of Tamar's sexual abuse at the hands of her brother, she remained desolate for the rest of her life. The original Hebrew word for "desolate" means ruined or wasted. Tamar became emotionally ruined, and isolated herself permanently. Many black women suffer from the "Tamar Complex." If it were an acronym, Tamar could very well stand for The Abused, Misused, And Refused. These women's lives have been tragically ruined and traumatically wasted by abusive men. For some, the pain exceeds their ability to cope and they end their own lives. Others live a socially reclusive life, learning never to trust men. They often remain single or get involved in a series of failed relationships. Still others turn to lesbianism to gain the love they now spurn and resent from men. The more educated African-American women become feminists and join the ranks of the controlling women who emerge as men-haters and male-bashers.

Whether it is the Jezebel syndrome, the cutting-words legacy, codependency, or the Tamar complex, there are strongholds particular to African-American women that are just as resistant as those found in African-American men.

CHAPTER FIVE

Strongholds Immobilizing African-American Youth

S trongholds in the African-American family sometimes are not simply related to gender, but are sometimes related to age, especially younger age members of the family. A brief look at some of the spiritual strongholds in African-American youth bear consideration.

THE TRIBALISM SYNDROME

Earlier we discussed the bloody warrior syndrome, one of the strongholds of black men. A dimension of this syndrome, namely "tribalism," represents one of the strongholds in African-American youth. Even though many of the Africans in the motherland are the same color, they still clash violently because of tribal differences. Consider the bloody, often deadly, conflicts between the Zulus and the African National Congress in South Africa. It is my opinion that gang violence among our African-American youth is just another form of the Afroism of tribalism. Young black brothers kill other young black brothers because they are from a different gang, that is, tribe. What we call gangs are in fact small urban tribes. One definition of tribe is "a group of persons having a common character, occupation, or interest." A gang is "a group of persons working or associated together." These definitions are very close in meaning. Satan's agenda is to pervert the young warrior nature of our African-American youth into tribalism—gang warfare, like Shaka Zulu tribalism—and get them to vent their rage on and destroy each other. Satan secretly fears that young warrior nature because he knows that if that rage is ever turned on him in the form of spiritual warfare, his days are numbered.

OUT-OF-WEDLOCK DEADLOCK

A second stronghold in African-American youth is what I call the "out-of-wedlock deadlock." Young African-American females are having babies at alarming rates. Two out of every three babies born out of wedlock are African-American and the majority of these births are to teen mothers. Children born in such families are the most likely to be premature, of low birth weight, learning disabled, and impoverished, become a perpe-trator or victim of crime, and be physically or sexually abused. The other frightening trend is that it appears the age of these mothers gets younger over time. Many of these teens are following the morality and birthing patterns of their mothers and grandmothers. In the words of Ezekiel, "as is the mother, so is her daughter" (Ezekiel 16:44). Many female teens grew up in homes where the mother had several boyfriends and lovers. This became an accepted practice.

NEGATIVE MUSIC

The devilish influence of certain kinds of pop, rock, and rap music creates a third stronghold for our African-American youth. Music is a powerful medium of influence, particularly in the lives of young African-Americans. Some feel that all that is uniquely their own is their music. Regrettably, several of these musical artists are tools of the enemy, unwitting vessels of Satan's strategy to kill, steal, and destroy African-American people. The music is used to promote abusive treatment against women, sexual immorality, perversion, violence, and rebellion against all authority. Moreover, a lot of the music videos feature symbolism and icons of Egyptology, African Voodoo, West Indian occultism, and satanic worship.

LOW SELF-ESTEEM

A fourth stronghold for the African-American youth is low self-esteem—black self-hate. Even though this is a book on spiritual strongholds related to the African-American family, it is virtually impossible to discuss the topic without discussing spiritual strongholds in whites. One primary stronghold in Caucasians is racism, which is defined as racial prejudice plus the political, economical, social, and even religious power to enforce it. When you are a minority group in a culture where one ethnic group places their own ethnicity as superior to all others and they control the means of media communication, there is a tendency for the minorities to think of themselves as less significant. In such an environment, ethnic self-hate will emerge. African-American youth are the early victims of the majority culture stronghold of racism, and strongholds breed strongholds. These youth enter into majority white schools thinking that they are not as smart or academically inclined.[1] Often they think that they aren't even as beautiful. Most of the African-American music videos of the females who are the love objects are very light-skinned, nearly white. Rarely is a dark brown woman used, and even more rarely is someone used that has Afroid features, such as kinky hair, full lips, and a broad nose. Ethnic self-hate is also partly the reason why African-American youth can so easily kill their own kind. Beyond the hold of the bloody warrior nature and tribalism on African-American youth, the bottom line is that black life is not valued in this country. Therefore, Dr. Alvin Poissant points out that it is easier for blacks to kill other blacks.[2]

PART TWO

Bringing the Strongholds Down

CHAPTER SIX

The Christian's Arsenal

We now turn our attention to overcoming strongholds. Strongholds are such resistant and formidable powers that only special weaponry can bring them down. However, we must understand what weaponry is available to Christians and how to effectively use it. Fortunately, we have some clues.

THE CHRISTIAN'S WEAPONS

"The weapons of our warfare are not carnal" (2 Corinthians 10:4). It is sad that Christians so often fail to understand this principle. So much time is lost and effort wasted because we resort to using fleshly means to address spiritual problems. All of our human ideas, whether derived from television talk shows, humanist philosophies, or our family are wholly inadequate. Nagging one's husband or shutting down on one's wife is nothing more than using carnal weapons.

Mighty Weapons

The Scripture reminds us that the weapons of our warfare rely on God's might to pull down strongholds. It is interesting that Satan's arsenal is mostly fiery darts or projectiles that are hurled at believers from a distance. Satan's weapons are primarily long-distance ones because he has respect for the power of Christians' weapons and prefers not to get close to them. God did not short-change believers on the fighting material end. It behooves a leader to equip his or her army with the best military hardware weapons their kingdom or government can afford. In the case of the army of the Lord, God has given His children the very best in terms of weaponry. No other fighting equipment in the entire universe has the power of a Christian's spiritual weapons. The weapons at our disposal are vastly superior to anything the devil can throw at us. Our weapons are mighty because they not only come *from* God, but they come *through* Him. His power empowers the weapons. His might is what makes them spiritually lethal. Comparing the Christian's arsenal to Satan's is like comparing an armored tank to a primitive spear. Our enemy is so outgunned that the Bible concludes that, as Christians, we are more than conquerors.

Effective Weapons

When God's army uses His weapons properly, they are effective. One can have military equipment with a lot of power, but not necessarily achieve the end result for which it was designed. Such is not the case with believers. The weapons we have are not only potent, they achieve the desired results, which is pulling down strongholds.

THE CHRISTIAN'S W–E–A–P–O–N–S

I have taken the word *weapons* and formed an acronym:

W—Word of God
E—Effective Prayer
A—Armor of God
P—Praise of God
O—Offerings of God
N—Name of God
S—Spirit of God

The Word of God

Our first and foremost offensive weapon is "**W**"—the Word of God, the sword of the Spirit (Ephesians 6:17). A person may purchase and use a Smith and Wesson revolver, a Colt firearm, or any other make of weapon. But the Smith and Wesson Company is best qualified to tell about the proper use of their revolver and the Colt company is best able to tell how to use and care for their gun. Soldiers that received M16s and M22s from the United States army had to be trained by the army in the proper use of that weapon because the firearms belong to the United States government.

Well, the Word of God belongs to the Spirit. It is His sword. We may use it, but it is the Spirit's weapon. Therefore it is the Holy Spirit who is best qualified to instruct Christians in its usage. In fact, the primary role of the Holy Spirit is to help believers to prepare for war. He is our fencing instructor in the proficient use of His sword. That is why our Lord said, "When the Comforter [*paraklete*; one called alongside to help] is come, ... even the Spirit of truth, ... he shall testify of me.... When he, the Spirit of truth, is come, he will guide you into all truth" (John 15:26; 16:13).

The second thing to be noted by the soldier who uses the sword of the Spirit is that it is sharper than any two-edged sword (Hebrews 4:12). This is not a sword with a single-edged blade. The sword that the writer of Hebrews had in mind was the Roman sword which had a straight two-edge blade that was rather broad, and its width nearly equaled the length from point to point. It was worn on the soldier's left side.[1] Hebrews says that this sword (Word) is "alive and full of power—making it active, operative, energizing and effective; it is sharper than any two-edged sword, penetrating to the dividing line of the breath of life (soul) and [the immortal] spirit, and of the joints and marrow [that is, of the deepest parts of our nature] exposing *and* sifting *and* analyzing *and* judging the very thoughts and purposes of the heart" (Hebrews 4:12 AMPLIFIED). The Word of God is the only sword that can cut to the inner core of a person's psyche and pierce down to one's soul, heart, and thoughts. This blade can go where no instrument has ever gone before.

When Jesus was tempted, He used this sword. The Scriptures tell us that He was led of the Spirit into the wilderness to be tempted of the devil (Matthew 4:4). In other words, the Holy Spirit, His sword-fighting teacher, directed Christ for some one-on-one sparring with Satan himself. Jesus was presented with three temptations. In each case, Jesus responded, "It is written ..." (verses 4, 7, 10). Do not think of Christ's responses as defensive maneuvers. They are, in fact, offensive counterattacks. Jesus' response is assertive and confrontational. Christ is not using a shield to protect Himself. He is fighting back with the sword of God's Word.

From the metaphor of the sword and the use of it modeled by the Lord Jesus, we learn something about this weapon. Swords were used on the *builders* of the strongholds, not the structure of the stronghold. They were used on people protecting the wall, not the walls themselves. The bringing down of the stronghold walls required another kind of weapon which we will discuss later. The Word, the sword, is used directly on Satan and his demons. Soldiers did not go around thrusting their swords at fortress walls. They did not use their blades on wall structures, they used them directly on the stronghold soldiers.

Prayer

Then what is used to bring down the walls of the stronghold barriers of the fortress? For that we need the second weapon, "**E**," the "effective prayer" of God's people.

In the book of James we read, "The effectual fervent prayer of a righteous man availeth much" (James 5:16). The Greek word "effectual" is *energeo*, which means to be active, efficient in working supplication, to be mighty in, to be operative, to put forth power, to produce an effect.[2] The Greek word for "fervent" is *zelos*, which means zeal, ardor, heat, or to be hot. True prayer or genuine supplication is prayer that has spiritual zeal and ardor and is effective and powerful.

The Ram

Prayer ought to be like two engines of war known as the battering ram and the crow. The ram was a simple machine, consisting of a metal head affixed to a beam which might be long enough to need 100–200 men to lift and impel it. When it was too heavy to lift, it was hung in a movable tower and became a wonderful engine of war. It was brought up to the

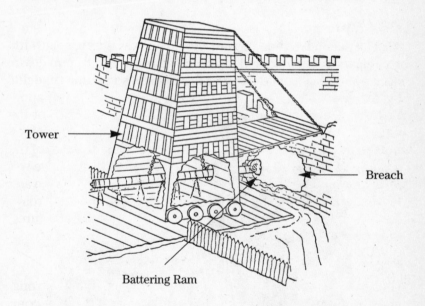

Tower

Breach

Battering Ram

walls by means of a bank.[3] The object of the battering ram was to make a breach (hole) in the wall of the stronghold or fortress.[4] The men using this instrument had to be patient and persistent. They couldn't cease ramming the walls. They had to continue until a breach was made. In the same way, we are admonished to pray without ceasing. If black Christians are going to bring down strongholds (arguments, imaginations) it will require the spiritual engine of war known as effectual, fervent, unceasing prayer directed specifically at those strongholds. The power to break down walls was not in the men who carried the ram, but rather in the ram itself. Every time Christians pray, they are hammering and ramming the walls of Satan's kingdom. That spiritual banging creates vibrations and thunderous noises that upset the evil principalities, throwing them out of sync.

The Scripture says our weapons are "mighty through God to the pulling down of strong holds" (2 Corinthians 10:4).

The Crow

The second engine of war, the crow, was a long spar with iron claws at one end and ropes at the other end to pull down stones and men from the top wall. Prayer is sometimes like the

crow. We are required to labor in prayer. Prayer is pushing in with the ram and pulling down the crow. These two engines symbolize two different kinds of prayer. The battering ram symbolizes intercession: a pushing action against the wall. The crow symbolizes supplication: an earnest request based on need. That is a pulling action. Prayer is both a pushing and a pulling action against strongholds. The sword of the Spirit and the battering ram and crow of effectual, fervent prayer are all offensive weapons. They directly assault the soldiers on the walls, as well as the walls themselves. Such weapons suggest that it is the Christian who should be on the offensive. If anyone should be defending himself, it should be the enemy. To be confrontational with Satan, however, is to invite attack from fiery darts—stone projectiles (attacks on the body), arrows (attacks on the mind), and javelins (attacks on the spirit).

Armor for Defense

Our third group of weapons is defensive, helping us survive Satan's attack. The defensive weapons are symbolized by the letter "**A**," which stands for the "armor of God."

The Helmet

The first piece of armor is the helmet of salvation. From the top of the walls of the stronghold, the enemy would drop stones, shoot arrows, and throw javelins. Armor became essential to those soldiers engaged in battering ram activity because they were on the front lines. They were close to the point of attack and most vulnerable to the fiery projectiles raining down on them from high on the fortress walls. Our helmet is referred to as the hope of our salvation (1 Thessalonians 5:8). It is Christ who is the hope of salvation who will protect our minds from the enemy's attack.

The Breastplate

Another significant piece of armor was the breastplate, worn to protect the heart. In the spiritual realm, it is called the breastplate of righteousness. It is the righteousness of Christ that protects our hearts, protects our emotions, and secures our feelings from Satan's assault. We cannot face the enemy with our own righteousness because all our righteousness is as "filthy rags" (Isaiah 64:6). To wrap my heart in filthy rags and go out to battle is like having no protection at all. Rags cannot stand up against stones, javelins, and arrows. We need the sturdy, durable metal of the righteousness of Christ. Satan is the accuser of the brethren. He sends out projectiles of accusation concerning one's character and one's past. He tries to make an issue of flaws, weaknesses, and imperfections. His goal is to make Christians appear unrighteous. I cannot use my own righteousness—which is filthy rags—as a breastplate, because the very thing I would use is the very thing the enemy would point out as evidence of my unrighteousness. Thus the filthy rags that are my protection become evidence of my filthy nature.

When I wear the true breastplate of righteousness, arrows of accusation and javelin thrusts that assault my character do not hurt me, because I do not stand or rest in my own righteousness, but in His righteousness in me, for me, to me, and through me. Arrows of accusation concerning my unrighteousness are intended to upset my heart and to create guilt and depression. If I become wounded in my heart, I am depressed and emotionally paralyzed. Obviously, I will not be able to do much fighting as a soldier.

The Girdle

The third piece of protective armor is the girdle of truth. It was the item from which the sword was suspended. It was made of leather and studded with metal plates. When the armor was light, the girdle was broad and fastened about the hips; otherwise it supported the sword slung like a scarf from the shoulder.[5] The girdle was no mere adornment but essential equipment. It was used to keep other pieces in place and to secure freedom of movement.[6] The word "truth" here means truthfulness, reality, sincerity, openness, and no deceit or disguises. The sword was suspended from the girdle, for without it the sword was not readily available for use. The symbolism here suggests that those who want to use God's Word must be people of sincerity and honesty, for without it everything falls apart and won't hang together. Our truthfulness and sincerity must be the basis on which we use God's Word. The sword will not be effective in the hands of deceivers. "It is God that girdeth me with strength. . . . [He] girded me with strength unto the battle" (Psalm 18:32, 39).

Shoes

A fourth important piece of armor was the shoes for the feet. The analogy here is of a Roman soldier's sandals, which were bound by thongs over the instep and around the ankle. The soles were thickly studded with nails.[7] These sandals were similar to the cleats that baseball and football players wear. They were designed to give the soldier firm footing in case of attack and to prevent slipping or falling. The Greek term for "preparation" is *hetoimazo*. It suggests establishment and a firm foundation. The Gospel, the Good News, must be the firm foundation on which we stand, giving us sure footing in battle. Many young African-Americans become born-again Christians but are never taught early and never receive basic foundational teaching in the Gospel—that is, the meaning of the death, burial, and resurrection of Jesus Christ. They are given strong-meat doctrines rather than the basic spiritual food of Christology (doctrine of Christ) and soteriology (doctrine of salvation). They are given teachings that are way above their heads on subjects like demonology (doctrine of demons), eschatology (doctrine of future things), angelology (doctrine of angels), and ecclesiology (doctrine of the church). These Christians never fully mature, and as a result they fall and surrender in battle because their feet were not properly shod. They did not receive a firm foundation in the Gospel on which to build. "Thou hast enlarged my steps under me, that my feet did not slip" (Psalm 18:36).

The Shield

The fifth piece of armor is the shield (*thureos*) of faith. This word refers to the oblong shield of the heavy infantry. Its dimensions were four feet high by two feet wide. It was sometimes curved on the inner side and covered with leather or other materials designed to extinguish the burning of a fiery arrow. It was large enough to protect a soldier from the assault of all the arrows shot at him. The shield actually protects the armor that protects the soldier. Soldiers who used the battering ram often had to help hold the ram with one hand while holding up the shield with the other. "Thou hast also given me the shield of thy salvation" (Psalm 18:35).

The Praise of God

The fourth spiritual weapon is characterized by the letter "**P**": the praise of God. In the Old Testament, Jehoshaphat "consulted with the people, [and] appointed singers unto the LORD, and that should praise the beauty of holiness" (2 Chronicles 20:21). The New International Version says, "After consulting the people, Jehoshaphat appointed men to sing to the LORD and to praise him for the splendor of his holiness as they went out at the head of the army, saying:'Give thanks to the LORD, for his love endures forever.'" As the singers began their praise, the Lord set ambushes against the invading men of Ammon, Moab, and Mount Seir, and they were defeated.

The original Hebrew words here for "praise" are *halal* and *yadah*. The first, *halal*, means to make a show, to boast, to rave, to celebrate, to be bright, to be clamorous and foolish, and to glory in. It is the source of "Hallelujah," a Hebrew expression of praise, which is found more than 160 times in the Old Testament.

The second word, *yadah*, means to give thanks, to laud and praise. It is a verb important to the language of worship and is found 120 times in the Old Testament. It carries the connotation of throwing or casting stones or arrows at something.

This physical connotation of the word *yadah* relates it to the engine of war known as the catapult. Ancients used two types: the "catapulta," which was used for throwing stones, and the "ballista" for launching arrows (see page 60). It was a very large stationary bow. Both of the engines had great powers to hurl projectiles. The catapult could throw stones weighing between 50 and 300 pounds. The darts and arrows of the ballista varied from small beams to large arrows. All of these engines were constructed on the principle of the crossbow.[8] Sometimes a mixture of sulfur was used on the projectiles to set the city on fire.[9] *Yadah* is the kind of praise that is a weapon against our spiritual enemy. Sometimes our battle against spiritual strongholds requires that we catapult praises to the Lord in the presence of the adversary. It throws the praises of God at Satan. This is the kind of praise that is done when you are about to face the devil in spiritual combat.

The Offerings of God

The fifth set of weapons is characterized by the letter "**O**." There are two kinds of offerings: first, God's offering to us; second, our offering to God. Christ offered Himself as one

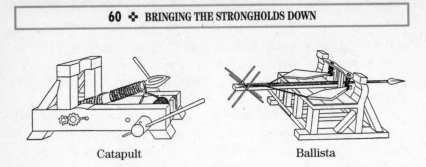

Catapult   Ballista

sacrifice for our sins forever and by this one offering He has perfected us forever (Hebrews 10:11–14). Through the offering of Himself through death, He destroyed him who had the power of death and delivered us, who through fear of death, were subject to bondage (Hebrews 2:14–15). The Greek word "destroy" here is *katurgeo*, meaning to abolish, to make of no effect, to render entirely useless, make void, to render inactive and ineffective, and to cause to cease.[10]

In ancient warfare, the weapon of choice to render an opponent's might and power useless and ineffective was the battle-ax. These narrow-headed axes could penetrate a helmet and crush the head of the enemy. Other axe blades were designed with wider edges to cut open the flesh where light armor or no armor was worn.[11] The Romans used a two-headed battle-ax called the "bipennis."[12] It was an awesome head-crushing weapon.

Christ's sacrificial offering in death served as God's battle-ax to crush Satan's head, which was precisely what God promised He would do to the enemy in Genesis (Genesis 3:15). God said that the seed of the woman (Christ) would bruise the head of the serpent (Satan). Calvary was the scene of God the Father swinging His battle-ax (Jesus Christ) at the head (power, might, and authority) of the enemy. Thus when Satan comes at us with his fiery javelins, we can block them with the shield of faith, and sometimes we pull out the battle-ax of Christ's offering of death to remind him that he is defeated. Just showing the battle-ax is victory enough, because the enemy knows what

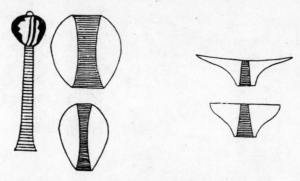

The mace consisted of a heavy, round object affixed to a handle. The ax (the right two objects) was similarly constructed. Both mace and ax were intended for hand-to-hand combat.

that weapon did to him at Calvary. Just the sight of it defeats him. So we lift up the battle-ax, meaning we lift up Jesus and His offering. Christ says, "If I be lifted up, I will draw all men unto me" (John 12:32). Lifting up the ax will cause men to be drawn forth, victory to be drawn out, and the enemy to withdraw.

God warned the city of Tyre that the King of Babylon would set battering rams against its walls and demolish its towers with his axes (Ezekiel 26:9). The symbol of the battle-ax is used regarding Cyrus, the King of Persia. Of him God says, "Thou art my battle axe and weapons of war: for with thee will I break in pieces the nations, and with thee will I destroy kingdoms" (Jeremiah 51:20). The battle-ax was indeed a formidable weapon used to crush the head of the opponent, cut his armor, and even smash and break down his towers.

Another meaning of the word "offering" has to do with what *I* give to God. When God accused His people of robbing Him in tithes and offerings (Malachi 3:8–11), he admonished them to bring all the tithes in the storehouse so that they could be blessed. He also says in verse 11, "And I will rebuke the devourer for your sakes, and he shall not destroy the fruits of your ground. . . ." Giving is a weapon, and our offerings are part of our arsenal against the enemy.

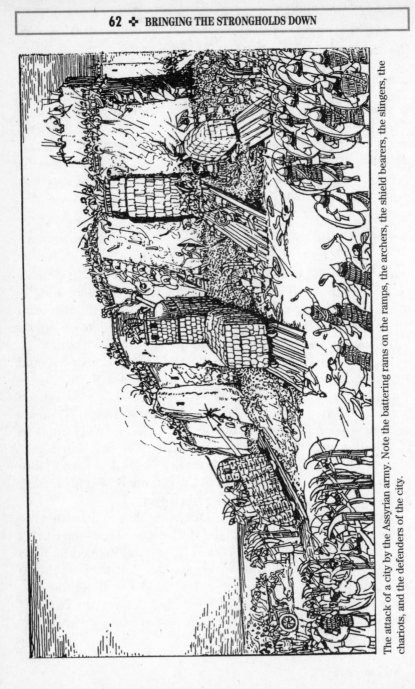

The attack of a city by the Assyrian army. Note the battering rams on the ramps, the archers, the shield bearers, the slingers, the chariots, and the defenders of the city.

The Name of God

Proverbs tells us that "The name of the LORD is a strong tower" (Proverbs 18:10). This brings us to the letter "**N**," which indicates our next weapon: the name of the Lord. The Hebrew word for tower is *migdalah*, used for the tower of a fortified city, a watchtower, a lofty platform, or a small fortress. Often an attacking army would build temporary walls (bulwarks) around its camp to prevent sneak attacks by the defenders of a stronghold.[13] Mobile towers from which archers could cover the advance of battering rams were used. The attacking army of a stronghold would use dirt ramps topped with rocks or logs to cover the sharp embankment of the lower walls to bring the rams and towers to the wall. These giant mobile towers gradually pushed up against the walls, and the earthen ramps enabled invaders to run up to and over the city walls.[14]

These towers with battering rams were highly effective.

Prayer (heaven's battering ram) is highly effective when combined with heaven's mobile tower, the name of Jesus. It was this spiritual engine of war that David used against the giant Goliath. Goliath was a human stronghold. He was high in stature, well fortified with armor, formidable in appearance, and intimidating in attitude. Yet, David announced to Goliath exactly what weapons he carried. "Thou comest to me with a sword, and with a spear, and with a shield: but I come to thee in the name of the LORD of hosts, the God of the armies of Israel, whom thou hast defied" (1 Samuel 17:45–46). Several things are significant about David's statement. First, David's chief weapon was the name of the Lord, a strong tower (Proverbs 18:10). When David mentioned the name of the Lord, the spiritual effect was that he immediately entered and was lifted high inside an invisible tower of power. Thus, the battle became the Tower of God versus the Hulk of a man.

We know that God's tower was far higher and more powerful. It was a man versus a powerful war machine. Usually, when a man challenges a machine, the man always comes out the loser. Goliath, even as big as he was, would have been able to take on a mobile defense tower. In modern terms, that would be like a Charles Atlas type soldier taking on a soldier inside a modern armored tank. My bet would be on the tank. Therefore, it was not David, but Goliath who was at the disadvantage, since the shepherd boy was safe, protected and elevated inside the Lord's strong tower, the name of the Lord. Naturally David had to look up to see the giant, but spiritually he was looking down on him. Sometimes circumstances in the African-American family seem to be like Goliath: huge, formidable, and menacing. We must remember, however, that although in this natural realm we may be looking up to the giant, in the spiritual realm we are safely seated in God's tower of protection. From such a high position giants look like midgets.

A second significant fact about David's announcement to Goliath is that David did not just invoke any name, but he specifically used the name of the Lord of Hosts which is the Hebrew word *Tsebaah*, meaning a mass company organized for war, a campaign battle, or warfare. David was really saying to the hulking Philistine, "I come to you in the name of the Lord of Hosts, who has organized a mass company of His soldiers for a campaign of battle." David was letting the giant know that Yaweh was the one who was the true commander of the Israelites, and that He had organized His hosts and was ready for war. Goliath unknowingly took on the army of God, not just of Israel.

A tower is a high and elevated structure. So is the name of Jesus. It is elevated high above all else. The Bible says that God has given Christ a name above every name (Philippians 2:9–11). Jesus said, "In my name shall they cast out devils" (Luke 16:17), and the disciples came back from a campaign rejoicing that these devils were subject to them through the name of Jesus (verse 17). Truly, the name of the Lord is a strong (high, mobile, and secure) tower.

The Spirit of God

Our final weapon is indicated by the letter "**S**," which stands for Spirit of God. The Lord said through the prophet Zechariah, "Not by might, nor by power, but by my spirit" (Zechariah 4:6). Moreover, one of the most common symbols for the Holy Spirit is fire. He has within Himself His own weapon, and it is a lethal weapon indeed. Fire is used in two ways to destroy strongholds. It is used to burn *down* the standing wall, and to burn *up* the remains after a city is besieged. The metaphor of fire associated with the Holy Spirit is seen in the following Scripture passages. "He shall baptize you with the Holy Ghost, and with fire" (Matthew 3:11 and Luke 3:16). "And there appeared unto them cloven tongues like as of fire, and it sat upon each of them" (Acts 2:3). "Our God is a consuming fire" (Hebrews 12:29). "When the Lord shall have washed away the filth of the daughters of Zion, and shall have purged the blood of Jerusalem from the midst thereof by the spirit of judgment, and by the spirit of burning" (Isaiah 4:4).

There are those who believe and teach that the fire is separate from the Holy Spirit, but the Scriptures above show that not to be true. If He is the Spirit of burning fire, then He comes with the fire. He is not separate from the fire, He is the fire.

Fire burns, consumes, and destroys. Thus strongholds not only have to be battered with the ram and pulled upon with the crow, but they also need to be burned by the fire of the Holy Spirit. Fire is a powerful weapon, often succeeding where other weapons fail. After the fall of the stronghold of Jericho, Joshua destroyed the city with fire (Joshua 6:24). The Bible also says that we are to walk in the Spirit, which means we are to walk in the fire of the Holy Spirit. Our enemy is hurling fiery darts at us and sometimes we have to fight fire with fire. Christians are admonished to "Quench not the Spirit" (1 Thessalonians 5:19). The Greek word for "quench" is *sbennumi*, meaning to extinguish as a flame. It is the same word used in Ephesians 6:16 when speaking of the shield of faith in reference to quenching all the fiery darts of the wicked one. Believers can, therefore, do things which extinguish the fire of the Holy Spirit. If this were not possible, there would be no need to warn us to "quench not." That is why as soldiers we want to avoid behavior that inhibits the flicker of the flame of God's Spirit.

The following table is given to summarize and conceptualize our weapons:

Letter	Acronym Meaning	Weapons Symbols	Type of Weapons	Soldier Example
W	Word of God Hebrews 4:12 Ephesians 6:17	Two-edged Sword	Short Range Offensive Against Enemy Soldier	Jesus in Battle of Wilderness Temptation Matthew 4:1–10
E	Effectual prayer of believer James 5:16 1 Timothy 2:1	Battering Ram Crow Bow & Arrows	Short & long Range Offensive Weapons and Engines of War for Strongholds	Daniel in Battle with Persia Daniel 10:12–13
A	Armor of God Ephesians 6:13–17	Helmet, Breastplate, Girdle, Shoes, Shield	Short & Long Range Defensive Against Enemy Soldier	Paul in Spiritual Warfare Ephesians 6:13–17
P	Praises of God 2 Chronicles 20:21–23	Catapult, Ballista	Long Range Offensive Engines of War Against Strongholds	Jehosophat's Singers in Battle Against Ammonites 2 Chronicles 20:21–23
O	Offering of God (His blood, powerful sacrifice) Hebrews 2:14–15; 10:11–14	Battle-Ax	Short Range Offensive Against Enemy Soldiers	Peter's Cutting Sermon Acts 2:36–37
N	Name of God 1 Samuel 17:45 Proverbs 18:10	Mobile Tower	Short Range Defensive & Offensive Engines of War Against Strongholds	David's Fight Against Goliath 1 Samuel 17:45
S	Spirit of God (Spiritual gifts) Matthew 3:1, Isaiah 4:4 1 Corinthians 12 Romans 12:6–8	Fire	Short & Long Range Offensive Weapon Against Soldiers & Strongholds	Upper Room Saints Acts 2:3

CHAPTER SEVEN

The Battle Plan: Part I

Familiarity with the weapons for battling strongholds is one thing; engaging in an effective battle using them is another story. No strategy will succeed on the battlefield that does not deal with the preparation and maturity of the soldiers themselves. To confront strongholds, one must have a warrior attitude and one must complete basic training.

GOOD SOLDIERS

What are the attitudes and qualities that make good soldiers? They are the following: endurance, exuberance, compliance, continuance, vigilance, belligerence, attendance, and proficiency.

Endurance

Soldiers must have an attitude of perseverance. They must accept the fact that suffering hardships and difficulties is part of warfare. They must be determined to go through it, no matter what. Basic training can be hard on new recruits, but the goal is to make them tough and hard. "Endure hardship like a good soldier" (2 Timothy 2:3 NIV).

Exuberance

Soldiers must develop some exuberance, or power. They must build up muscle, develop strength, and condition the mind and body. God's army is to "be strong in the Lord, and in the power of his might" (Ephesians 6:10). All who plan on confronting a stronghold had better build themselves up and empower themselves spiritually beforehand.

Compliance

Good soldiers must be obedient to their commanding officer and do whatever that officer commands. Christ is our commanding officer. He is referred to as the "Captain of our Salvation." When Joshua was about to lay siege to Jericho, he had an encounter with a celestial angelic being, and said to him: "'Are you for us or for our enemies?' 'Neither,' he replied, 'but as commander of the of the army of the LORD I have now come.' Then Joshua fell facedown to the ground in reverence, and asked him, 'What message does my Lord have for his servant?' The commander of the LORD's army replied, 'Take off your sandals, for the place where you are standing is holy.' And Joshua did so" (Joshua 5:13–15 NIV).

Joshua recognized the real leader of his army and obeyed Him. That's the mark of a good soldier.

Continuance

Good soldiers are consistent in the fight; determined to stand their ground no matter what. Having put on the armor and done all that is possible to prepare, they stand (Ephesians 6:13).

Vigilance

Good soldiers are watchful and vigilant, always aware of their surroundings and always looking for a possible ambush (1 Peter 5:8–9). Believers are admonished to "be sober, be vigilant [watchful], because your adversary the devil, as a roaring lion, walketh about, seeking whom he may devour." Lions generally stalk their prey and depend on the element of surprise to make their attack.

Belligerence

Belligerence is a warlike attitude, a readiness to fight one's enemy. A soldier that wants no surprise attacks must be on the lookout. We are encouraged to "fight" the good fight of faith (1Timothy 6:12).

Attendance

Good soldiers must attend to the business of the war and be focused on winning the battle. Timothy says that "no man that warreth entangleth himself with the affairs of this life; that he may please him who hath chosen him to be a soldier" (2 Timothy 2:4). Soldiers cannot afford to have divided loyalties or divided focus, for then they are double-minded. A double-minded person is unstable, and an unstable person is an undependable soldier. This kind of soldier will not be vigilant, not ready for attack, will not have his heart in the fight, will go AWOL, deserting in the heat of the battle.

Proficiency

Proficient soldiers are very familiar with and skilled in the use of all the weapons and equipment. They practice with the weapons often and take good care of the artillery. Honing their skills becomes a major focus for such warriors. They look for something that will give them the advantage in battle.

GOOD TRAINING

This brings us to the training of a soldier. King David spoke from experience: "He teacheth my hands to war, so that a bow of steel is broken by mine arms" (Psalm 18:34). "Blessed be the LORD my strength, which teacheth my hands to war, and my fingers to fight" (Psalm 144:1). Solomon reinforced the suggestion: "Every purpose is established by counsel, and with good advice make war" (Proverbs 20:18). "A wise man is strong; yea, a man of knowledge increaseth strength. For by wise counsel thou shalt make thy war: and in the multitude of counselors there is safety" (Proverbs 24:5–6). "Wisdom is better than weapons of war" (Ecclessiastes 9:18).

What all these passages have in common is the emphasis on teaching knowledge and wisdom as it relates to warfare. The purpose of training is to provide the wisdom and counsel necessary to face one's opponent. The word "teacheth" (Psalms 18:34 and 144:1) is the Hebrew word *lamad*, meaning to goad or to strike with a rod. The desired goal is to discipline, chastise, accustom, or cause one to learn. The word carries with it the idea of learning through discipline. God uses suffering to teach us discipline and to train us for warfare that we may learn obedience. Even our Lord, who is our captain in warfare, was subject to this kind of discipline. "Though he were a Son, yet learned he obedience by the things which he suffered" (Hebrews 5:8).

If one were to single out those who have gone through military training, one would surely find individuals who viewed their training as suffering. That is the reality of the military's stringent demands, the biting reprimands from drill sergeants, and the constrictive boundaries of military rules. In a similar way, God sometimes appears to be the ultimate drill sergeant. He is determined to teach us how to war.

As the word *lamad* implies, the Lord goads us like oxen. The goad was a sharp stick—often shod with iron—used as a stimulus. It was used to discipline oxen, keep them in line, and force them to go the direction their master wanted them to go. There are times as part of God's discipline training that He goads His children into submission. He intentionally and strategically uses the sufferings of life as His goading rod. Any African-American Christian trying to bring down family strongholds who has not experienced and successfully endured the discipline of God will come away from the battlefield a frustrated and defeated soldier.

BOOT CAMP CHECKLIST

Are you trained and ready for battle? Are the people you are considering as part of your spiritual army trained and ready for battle? Prayerfully consider and answer "yes" or "no" to the following questions:

_____ Are you willing to see this spiritual battle through until the very end? Even when things get challenging and tough?

_____ Are you depending on the Lord's power to carry out this military strategy or are you depending on your own abilities?

_____ Are you willing to obey Christ's instructions regardless of what others might say or in spite of the way you may feel?

_____ Are you on the alert for Satan's schemes and tactics to discourage you from doing this? Will you continue to be watchful for him and other fleshly desires tempting you not to obey Christ?

_____ Are you ready to fight? Do you want to tear down Satan's strongholds?

_____ Are you trusting God with your own personal dilemmas? Are you able to fight on behalf of someone else?

_____ Are you familiar with biblical weapons of warfare? Have you any experience with pulling down strongholds in your own life?

If you can honestly answer yes to most of these questions, you are ready to leave boot camp and prepare for serious battle. If you answered no, don't give up. Do what is necessary for you to grow and mature to the point of being ready for a battle like this. (For example: ask a mature Christian to disciple you. Go through or start to attend some Bible studies on Christian growth and maturity. Choose a more mature Christian to lead and administrate the battle and make yourself an encourager and helper.)

CHAPTER EIGHT

The Battle Plan: Part II

Proverbs reminds believers that it is "by wise counsel thou shalt make thy war" (Proverbs 24:6). This word "counsel" in the Hebrew is *tachbuwlah*, which means steerage, guidance, a plan, rule, prudence, or cunning counsel. That kind of counsel comes from God through His written Word. The apostle Paul exhorted young Timothy, "This charge I commit unto thee, son Timothy, according to the prophecies which went before on thee, that thou by them mightest war a good warfare" (1 Timothy 1:18). The young pastor was exhorted here to be mindful of the fact that it would be by God's specific instructions by which he would be able to war a good warfare.

The Scriptures are God's war plan, His divine military strategy, His prophetic "how-to manual" to do battle. Hence, most training is part action, part instruction, part hearing, and part doing. Once an army has completed basic training they are ready to implement the war plan which will be given them by their superiors.

THE TARGET FAMILY

When choosing a target family, look for the "Rahab Type" of family. To understand what is meant by this we have to understand the biblical personality of Rahab described in Joshua

(Joshua 2). She was an Amorite woman who resided in Jericho, in the land of Canaan. Canaanites were descendants of Canaan, who was the youngest son of Ham, the patriarch of the people of color. Rahab, a descendant of Ham, was most likely a dark-complexioned woman. If Rahab were living today she would probably be classified as a black woman or member of the black race. She was a known prostitute in Jericho with a certain degree of notoriety. Yet, five things made Rahab and her family different from the other Canaanite inhabitants. When seeking a target family, look for these characteristics.

A Key Influential Member

The "Rahab Type" family will usually have a key influential member who is able to mobilize the other members of the family to action. This person's role in the family is that of a "savior." This role fell to Rahab. She was the rescuer or savior of her family. She had a tremendous amount of power among her relatives.

A Fear of God

This key influential member will be kind and receptive to the servants of God and will have a fear of God. It is true, Rahab was a prostitute and she lived within a stronghold; however, she still had a fear of the true God. "I know, the LORD hath given you the land, and that your terror is fallen upon us, and that all the inhabitants of the land faint because of you . . . for the LORD your God, he is God in heaven above, and in the earth beneath" (Joshua 2:9, 11).

A Desire for Deliverance

The key member, although within a stronghold, will be desirous of deliverance from that stronghold. "Now therefore, I pray you, swear unto me by the LORD, since I have shewed you kindness that ye will also shew kindness unto my father's house, and give me a true token: And that ye will save alive my father, and my mother, and my brethren, and my sisters, and all that they have, and deliver our lives from death" (Joshua 2:12–13). Rahab wanted freedom not only for herself, but also for her family.

Cooperativeness

The key member will cooperate with the advancing army and do what he or she is told that will bring about deliverance, "Then she let them down by a cord through the window" (Joshua 2:15). Rahab risked her personal safety and security to help the spies and therefore help rescue herself and her family.

Hopefulness

The influenced member will patiently wait for deliverance and display a "scarlet cord" of hope (Joshua 6:22–23). The destruction of Jericho was not merely the possessing of the land of Canaan. God also wanted to free a very important family in Canaan. The walls of this stronghold had to come down in order for Rahab and her family to be released. This family had to come out of this stronghold because of the special contribution the key member would make to the ultimate salvation that God would bring to mankind.

Rahab was no ordinary woman. She became one of the great-grandmothers of the Lord Jesus Christ. "Salmon the father of Boaz, whose mother was Rahab" (Matthew 1:5 NIV). Here, in the genealogy of the Lord Jesus Christ, the Hamitic woman, is listed this woman of color. Rahab was delivered to become the matriarch of the deliverer. She was saved to be part of the bloodline of the Savior. Like Rahab, there are other Hamites, people of color, from African-American families who are bound within a stronghold. They are holding together with their scarlet thread of hope, waiting for the army of God to tear down the walls, defeat the resisters, and rescue them. The rest of this chapter explains a strategic plan to make sure this is done.

SIEGE WARFARE

We will now review the elements of the warfare strategy one based on the ancient format called "siege warfare." We will discuss siege elements: assessment, arrangement, advancement, encirclement, development, engagement, and enslavement.

Assessment

This assessing was primarily accomplished through the use of spying. Spying is the secret observance of your enemy's strengths and weaknesses. Spiritual warfare against the strongholds in African-American families will require some spiritual spying. Observations and documentation of the strongholds will need to be made without the family members you are considering to target being aware of your observances. Part of the assessment process is identifying the Jericho, the main stronghold. Next one must determine the foundations of the stronghold, whether they are fear, anger, pride, idolatry, lust, or any other stronghold you might observe. One must determine how high and how thick the walls are. Who are the ruling principalities? What are the dynamics of the strongholds? What are the resistant arguments of the family members which keep them bound? What are the root causes? How does it manifest itself? How well defended are these persons? One must identify the arguments.

The following are just a few common resistant/dominant walls of argument in African-American people.

Black Men	Black Women	Black Youth
	Relationships	
You can't trust black women.	All black men are dogs	My parents don't deserve obedience.
Black women are mean, spiteful, and they use you.	Women must take charge and never let a man control them.	
Women are only good for having babies and cooking.	I can't live without this man.	
You have to slap a woman around every now and then.	He beats me, but he's a good man.	
You have to love them and leave them.		
	Morality and Character	
It's all right to have more than one woman.	You've got to sleep with a man in order to get him.	Everybody else is doing it and so can I.
Drugs and alcohol are not that bad.		I will do whatever I want.
The only thing that is important is what you do for yourself.		I will hurt others before I hurt myself.
	Religion	
I am God.	Following my horoscope is all right to engage in and to use to find a mate.	There is no God.
The Bible is the white man's religion.	Eastern Star is a good thing.	
	Islam is the black man's religion.	
	The church is full of hypocrites.	
	Christianity is a crutch for weak black folks.	
	The Masons are a good thing.	

To determine if you have done an adequate job of assessing the target family, go through the following checklist.

Assessment Checklist

_____ Selected your targeted family

_____ Observed the behavior of the family in as many settings as you are able and wrote down what you have observed

_____ Looked for the "Jericho," the primary stronghold

_____ Determined its foundation (fear, lust, anger, pride, or idolatry) and type (Nimrod, Jezebel, bloody warrior, etc.)

_____ Determined the ruling king; demonic spirits at work (spirits of lust, anger, etc.)

_____ Determined strength of the walls (the resistant arguments of the family) and wrote them down

_____ Completed the "Family Assessment sheet" on page 104

Arrangement

After the assessment, we move to the second element of siege warfare, which is arrangement or military action plan. Your assessment should be completed and you should know the name of the stronghold you have targeted for defeat, the name of the ruling principality, the foundational sin on which it stands, the weapons at the enemy's disposal, the thickness of the walls (arguments and rationalizations), and the strengths and weaknesses of what primary spiritual weapons that will be employed.

The next step will nail down the time you will commence and a list of warrior prospects broken down by long-range type, medium-range type, and close-range type.

Unity

To bring down family strongholds it will require an army of people willing to work together to achieve victory. Therefore, we must not try to act as a one-man army. The Bible says, "*We* wrestle [not "*I* wrestle"] ... against principalities ... powers ... rulers of the darkness ..." (Ephesians 6:12). We will need to solicit the help of others. A good place to start to build this army is among the nuclear family itself. Seek out those members who are born-again and have gone through the discipline of God. From there we can radiate out to extended family members and in-laws with whom we have positive relationships. We can radiate further out to close friends of the family. A church setting or a Bible study group can also implement this prayer strategy. We will discuss this in more detail later.

It is crucial that the members of this spiritual military team be selected carefully and prayerfully. This army must be unified and understand its ultimate goals and not to be prone to striving against each other. Once the experienced, spiritually trained army is assembled, they need to be organized according to spiritual abilities and maturity.

Gifts

Power and energy are given to believers in the form of spiritual gifts. These special abilities are mentioned in 1 Corinthians 12:1–12, 28–31; Romans 12:6–8; Ephesians 4:11. When these gifts are correctly in operation they can be powerful weapons. They are Holy Spirit fire at work *in* and *through* us. This is why it is very important to organize your warriors according to gifts. Taking the sum total of all the gifts mentioned in the verses of Scripture above, the gifts to spiritual warriors could look like the following:

Spiritual Warrior Type	Representation	Comparable Gifts
Long Range		
Archers	Out of town individual prayer warriors	Faith, languages, serving,
Catapult Team	Out of town team of praisers	Mercy, giving
Ballista Team	Out of town team of prayers	Serving, faith, giving, languages
Medium Range		
Ram Team and Tower Archers	Main intercessory prayer group, close individual prayer warriors	Faith, mercy, languages, language interpretation, serving
Crow Team	Main supplication prayer group	Faith, mercy, languages, language interpretation
Team Captain	Leader of group	Ruling, administration, faith, mercy, languages, exhortation
Close Range/Ground Infantry		
Swordsmen	Those skilled in using the Word	Pastors, teachers, apostles, evangelist, exhortation, word of wisdom, word of knowledge
Axmen	Those skilled exercising the power of God and blood offering of Christ	Prophets, discerning of spirits, miracles, healings

Unfortunately, the subject of spiritual gifts has been a source of division among Christians. This was never the intent of the Lord. Rather than further the controversy I suggest that churches and individuals address the issue of gifts from whatever their particular doctrinal stance may be. What's important is that they are recognized and utilized for God's glory. Spiritual gifts are powerful weapons in the battle to tear down strongholds. When you have Christians who exercise their spiritual gifts fueled by spiritual fruit, they are like ancient warriors setting torches to fortresses, burning down the walls of their enemies, setting them ablaze. Such power is irresistible.

Formation

The following formation is suggested as a way to organize the army:

Long-Range Soldiers

The long-range soldiers are those who by nature of distance or relationship cannot be on the front lines but will willingly participate from a distance. I call these soldiers the catapult team, the archers, and the ballista team.

Catapult

The catapult workers are those family members and friends who live out of town who will participate by constantly praising God for your victory, thus hurling the stones of prayer and praise from a distance. This kind of praise is called *yadah*. It is praise of God using the catapult (stone hurler) and ballista (arrow shooter) to shoot at the enemy. Both are long-distance weapons. Persons for this role should be those with a love and anointing in the area of praise and worship. In a church setting the worship leader, worship team members, singers, and musicians should be considered.

Archers

The archers consist of individual prayer warriors. They are those who are away or distant but who will in their individual prayer time target a specific demon to pray about.

Ballista

The ballista team is a major group. Unlike individual archers who shoot out small individual arrows, the ballista requires a small group of men to operate it. The ballista symbolizes those small prayer groups and gatherings who pray together and send out one big arrow of prayer. For example, Jehoshaphat sent out singers before the army to praise the Lord.

Medium-Range Soldiers

The medium-range soldiers consist of the battering ram team and crow team. They are the family members and friends living nearby who agree to participate. They will be on the front lines and close to the attack. They are key prayer warriors who will focus on the walls of the family strongholds. They are the members of primary prayer groups who will meet on a regular basis. They will commit to pray without ceasing.

Battering Ram

The ancient battering ram required several men to operate it as a group effort of relentless and consistent banging on the walls until a breach occurred. Their main goal was to break the walls of the enemy fortress. The rammers are those people with the ministry of intercession. For them, intercessory prayer is as natural as breathing. They are the type who will spend hours in prayer, even praying through the night. They believe in praying through and breaking through.

Crow

The crow team are supplicators, who, like rammers, are relentless in prayer. The difference is that while the rammers (pushers) are characterized by their boldness and aggressiveness in prayer, the supplicators (pullers) are characterized by their earnestness, compassion, and burden to see the need dealt with. They often will weep for people. The pullers of the crow had to hold on tightly to the ropes attached to the weapon. The pulling could become burdensome and agonizing. In the same ways, supplicators are a group of prayer warriors who will agonize in prayer and feel the burden for deliverance. They implore God and beseech heaven until stronghold stones topple and the enemy falls. It is the duty of the long-range catapult and ballista workers and the archers to provide cover for the rammers and crows. They long-range target soldiers on the walls who will attack the mid-range rammers and crows. Those closer to the battle will be the ones to encounter the brunt of the enemy's attack. Therefore, rammers and crows must be well armed. They need to be forewarned that the spiritual defenders of the strongholds will target them, so they can be ready and fully outfitted.

Close-Range Soldiers

Once the defenders on the wall are defeated by the archers, ballista, and catapult team workers, and once the rammers and crows have done sufficient damage to the walls to allow entrance, the next group of soldiers—the swordsmen and axmen—can go in and do hand-to-hand combat with the enemy inside the stronghold.

Swordsmen

The swordsmen are those skilled in the Word of God. They know how to rightly divide the Word. They are well trained in knowing when and how to use Scripture. They typically are your ministers, Bible teachers, Bible scholars, and avid students of the Word. They will meet face-to-face with family members to give evangelical witness and share the faith.

Axmen

The axmen are those skilled in blood sacrifice of Christ. They use the power of the Holy Spirit to identify, confront, and cast out devils. They are the exorcists of the body who know how to use the battle-ax on the head of the enemy. The symbol of a head signifies rulership, authority, government, and power. These individuals skillfully use the power of God and blood of Christ to break the authority of the enemy. Frequently, those ancient axmen and swordsmen were rolled up to the wall in mobile towers that were as high as the stronghold walls themselves. Walking platforms were extended from the tower to the top of the wall, allowing the swordsmen and axmen, protected by shields and protective armor, to walk across and engage the enemy under the protection of the tower archers. The swordsmen fought in hand-to-hand combat. Besides the swordsmen and axmen, other swordsmen and axmen fought on the ground. Therefore, there was a battle going on in high places as well as on the ground.

Coordinating Captain

To implement the warfare strategy in this book requires a leader who is spiritually mature, has exceptional organizational skills, has the time to implement the plan, and is able to contact and utilize persons from both the local and outside areas. In some cases, it may mean you will have to take a step back to allow someone else to actually function as organizer of the plan or recruiting a co-captain. To see if you or the person you are considering for the coordinating captain position is qualified, answer these questions:

Coordinating Captain Checklist

_____ Have you thoroughly read this book?
_____ Do you know at least twelve mature Christians willing to pray (local and outside of town)? Are you capable of pulling these people together to form a warrior team?
_____ Can you adequately select, orient, and motivate the team?

_____ Are you close enough to the targeted family to spy out and gather enough information for a warfare action plan?

_____ Do you have the time, ability, and resources to put out a newsletter, mail all important information, make calls, stay in touch with the prayer team leaders, and stay in touch with the war action?

_____ Can you plan and implement a pre-victory rally and post-victory celebration?

_____ Can you secure covenants of participation from all the members involved?

_____ Are you willing to go above and beyond the call of duty to ensure the success of the endeavor?

_____ Will you keep information confidential?

_____ Are you willing to cooperate and submit to a pastor?

If you or the person you are considering can answer yes to these questions then you have found the best person for the coordinating captain position. If you recognize that you personally cannot handle this top administrative job, pray and ask the Lord to show you who may be able to take on this important responsibility. Then, talk with them personally and ask them to pray about the possibility of serving as captain.

Recruiting the Team

Once the coordinating captain is secured, he or she proceeds to contact prospective warriors. Initially, the captain will need to converse briefly with each prospective team member by phone to explain what you are doing and elicit their involvement. Indicate to each prospective warrior that a letter, job description, and covenant statement will be forthcoming. (See sample letters, job descriptions, and covenant statement in appendix 1.) The letter explains your plan and why you solicit their involvement, and asks them to reply by a certain date. You can also include a request for financial support for the (spiritual) war chest.

You should have a list of alternative team members if your first choice prospects are unable to participate. This alternative list also serves as your reserve replacements if one of the soldiers is wounded and has to be taken out of the battle.

Each letter needs to be followed up by another phone call. Personal contact usually is a good idea, if it is possible. This second contact with the prospective warrior should secure their commitment to the idea and invite them to a meeting to thoroughly explain the plan and appoint positions.

Start your prospective warrior selection with your catapult and ballista workers and archers (long-distance praise and intercession). You need a leader for each small group of prayers—a prayer group that is already established. The only person in the group you need to contact then is the leader, and that person will alert the rest of the group to what is happening.

Where no group exists, it may be necessary for someone to take responsibility to form one. Such a person will need to be thoroughly oriented as to what they have to do and when they have to do it.

Pre-Victory Celebration

Once you have received an affirmative reply from your participants, call a meeting with those who are in the local area to further orient them to the battle plan, affirm commitments (by collecting covenant sheets), give an opportunity for participants to get to know one another, and have a time of prayer and pre-victory celebration. Everyone should already be familiar with their job description and have a general idea about the plan.

The two local core groups of rammers and crows should be appointed at this meeting. The swordsmen and ax warriors should also be secured. This book, *Breaking Strongholds in the African-American Family*, should be passed out to those who may not have it. Also, team members should be given a list of Scriptural passages to read on spiritual warfare, victory, triumph, and overcoming the enemy to help them think like a soldier. (For example: the book of Joshua, certain battles of David and some of Israel's kings, and victory Scriptures such as James 4:7; Philippians 4:13; 1 John 4:4.)

Announce that the coordinating captain will let them know when the battle will commence. The team begins their efforts on the same day and at the same time. The newsletter may be used to give the battle signal to begin the fight. (A relevant military name, such as "Battle Cry," "Christian War Chronicle," "Banner of Victory," Warrior Notes," or "Soldiers of Triumph" may be used as a suggested title for the newsletter.)

Plan other meetings. One might be a pre-battle victory rally, including all the local warriors. Encourage the out-of-town teams to do the same. Another meeting might just be for point of contact or encouragement. The final meeting should be a victory celebration.

At the pre-victory meeting have a time of singing, worship, and praise. Sing songs pertaining to battle, victory, and war. For example: "I Am on the Battlefield for My Lord," "Victory Is Mine," "Onward, Christian Soldiers." If possible, print the words to these songs and allow team members to take them with them to sing in preparation for and during the battle. This might be a good time for someone to bring a brief message about a victorious battle in the Bible or share a brief testimony about a family that was saved through persistent prayer.

Advancement

After the assessment of the enemy and the arrangement of an action plan, the third element of siege warfare is advancement. There comes a point where you must implement the plan, be a doer of the Word, and move forward. In warfare, Christians are called not to retreat, but to advance. They are not to wait for the enemy to attack but should initiate the battle. Believers must advance and move toward our target with faith and confidence, remembering that the battle ultimately is not our battle, but the Lord's (2 Chronicles 20:15). The ten spies Moses sent out came back with an evil report. Gideon lost the majority of his army, who deserted him in fear; the Israelites who faced Goliath took a coward's response to the giant; all of them were defeated because they forgot this fact. The battle was not theirs—*but the Lord's*! We should advance knowing not only is it His battle, but He has already fought it and given us the victory. "[God] disarmed the principalities and powers ranged against us and made a bold display *and* public example of them, in triumphing over them in Him *and* in it [the cross]" (Colossians 2:15 AMPLIFIED).

The word "spoiled" used in the King James Version is *apekdu*, meaning to strip off or disarm. The word "show" is *deigmatizo*, which is a rare verb translated "displayed" or make a spectacle of. The word is relating a familiar scene for the Roman army of a conqueror returning to Rome and leading the captured kings and warriors in chains in his triumphal procession.[1] This is what Christ did at Calvary. Jesus victoriously made a spectacle of the enemy in defeat to indicate that war was fought and won at Calvary. Therefore, we have the victory already. The major demonic principalities have been vanquished. This is why we can say, "Thanks be to God, which giveth us the victory" (1 Corinthians 15:57). It is with this insurance of truth that we have an assurance of heart to advance upon Satan's kingdom in confidence and faith. "This is the victory that overcometh the world, even our faith" (1 John 5:4).

Advancement Checklist

_____ Get the signal from your captain (Jesus) and pass it on to the other warriors.

_____ Call a fast on the part of all the soldiers. Fasting prepares the soldiers and enhances the weapons of prayer. Our Lord said that some demonic forces will not move until fasting is coupled with prayer. Have the soldiers read the following passages during their time of fasting: Matthew 17:21; 6:16–18; 1 Corinthians 7:5; Isaiah 58:3–6; Joel 1:14; 2:15; Psalms 35:13; 69:10.

_____ Plan a going-out-to-battle victory rally and invite all the local warriors. Encourage the out-of-town team to do the same.

_____ Help and encourage the warriors to visualize themselves as soldiers in battle, help the ballista team envision themselves hitting the target with stones, help the tower archers imagine themselves in the mobile tower. Do the same for the rest of the team. It might help to use pictures of the weapons, act out the battle in a drama, view clips from old movies that use these instruments of war (*Masada* or *Ben-Hur*) or have someone draw a picture of a soldier ready for battle (preferably an African-American).

_____ Encourage the team to advance into battle with singing. Use some of the songs mentioned earlier.

Encirclement

The fourth element of siege warfare following our advancement is encirclement. In ancient siege warfare, a line of circumvallation constructed out of trees surrounding the vicinity was drawn around the place. This line not only cut off the besieged, but it also served as a base of operation.[2] This means that family strongholds must be attacked from every side; front and rear, north, south, east, and west. You want to hem in your enemy. This is why you need a circle of spiritual warriors who will surround the targeted stronghold with prayer, praise, and fire in the Spirit. Therefore, you should select people from the corners and direction from the surrounding neighborhoods, cities, and states. Make sure your catapult warriors and archers are from the surrounding areas of the targeted family with the stronghold you are trying to destroy. Allow no point of escape, permit no breach in your circle and give no place to the devil.

Development

Development is the fifth element of siege warfare. Once the enemy is surrounded, the besieging army begins to build mounds. They elevate the occupied ground around the strongholds. Towers will be built on these mounds and catapults prepared for hurling large darts and stones.[3] Development is the building of the mounds and towers, and establishing the catapults (stone hurlers) and ballista (giant arrow hurlers).

This element of warfare symbolizes the fact that those who participate in the war must be built up and elevated. Their spirits and morale must be lifted. They need to get up and stay up. Building the tower is likened to encouraging your long-distance warriors that whatever they do, do it in the name of the Lord (Colossians 3:17). They are to consistently use His name as they develop and prepare themselves for battle. Exhort them by letter or by phone to call upon His name (Psalm 105:1), give thanks to His name (Psalm 106:47), to lift the victory banner in His name (Psalm 20:5), and to recognize that there is help in His name (Psalm 124:8). For as stated earlier, His name is a strong tower. As your archers and catapult workers operate under His authority, they are gradually building a strong tower. They will be more effective in the hurling of their projectiles from a high position.

Engagement

Once the engines of war are developed and assembled and the enemy has been surrounded on every side, it is time for the next element of siege warfare: engagement. The captain is the one who will give the signal to attack. He determines the timing of the assault. Christ is our captain and commander. We must begin when He tells us to begin. He knows the optimal moment for attack. Once we get the orders from Him in prayer to go forward, this signal then must be relayed to all the other warriors until it passes completely around the circle. This is why you need officers in charge of each group who will pass the word to soldiers under them. Your prayer and praise leaders are these officers. It is good to have the battle commence on the same day and hour. They can be informed by phone and/or letter when the battle will begin.

In engagement, the attacking army initiate the battle by going on the offensive. Remember, we don't wait for the enemy to attack us, we attack him first. Two things happen virtually simultaneously. The battering ram crews, usually inside mobile towers with rams, move in close to the walls to begin a surrounded assault, and several crow pullers surround the walls with crows and begin pulling on them from various sides. The attack on the stronghold has begun! The defenders on the wall fortify themselves and defend the strongholds by hurling rocks, javelins, and arrows at the attackers. While the rammers and crow pullers assault the walls directly, the archers and catapulters provide cover for them, directing their projectiles at the stronghold defenders.

Your core prayer group, who will meet with you on a regular basis, will be at the front lines of the battle. They are your rammers and crow pullers. You could have several ram teams and several crow teams working on various sides of the stronghold walls. Now one can see why a circle of long-distance coverage is necessary to protect those at the cutting edge of the fight.

It is important to remember that siege war is not a quickly won battle. In ancient times it took weeks, months, and in some cases years. Today, we live in a "do it quick" world of minute rice, fast food restaurants, overnight express, and fax. We like things quick and instantaneous. Unfortunately, this attitude has been carried over into some elements of Christian doctrine. We want it done now. If we say the right religious phrase, make the correct confession, declare the proper Scripture, or offer the appropriate religious cliché, some believe that all of their problems will be solved in a moment. Such teaching has contributed to a generation of pleasure seeking, "give me what I want," lazy Christians, who don't want to work or fight for anything. These believers are often shocked to find out that some things don't move just because they say move. They have forgotten that the Bible does not say to put on your whole leisure suit, but rather, put on the whole armor of God. We are talking about conflict and struggle.

Some Christians are even amazed to find out when they take the offensive and attack, the enemy will fight back. The bottom line is that to engage the enemy means to wrestle with spiritual wickedness in high places. The good news is our weapons are more than up to the task, our war has been made easier by the victory won by our Lord at Calvary. If we have the proper soldier attitude, use our weapons effectively, are relentless in the fight, and follow the battle plan, we will eventually be rewarded with victory. The walls will be destroyed, ruling principalities defeated, and defenders beaten.

Engagement Checklist

_____ Activate your long-distance warriors; first, the individual prayer warriors (archers), then the ballista team (distant prayer groups), and afterward the catapult team (praise and prayer group).

_____ The next step is to activate the tower archers (individual prayer warriors) and at the same time mobilize the battering ram teams and the crow teams.

_____ Make sure your warriors are given specific instructions. Archers, catapult, and ballista teams should all be given the family name and the specific principality they will be praying against.

_____ The battering ram and crow teams need to be given the name of the family, the foundation of the stronghold, and the specific stronghold arguments and reasonings (walls) they will be praying against.

_____ Tower archers should be supplied with the name of the family and specific principalities and evil spirits to target for prayer.

_____ Warriors should be given clear instructions not to disclose the names or circumstances of the family.

_____ The battle must continue until there is a breach in the wall. When the family becomes less resistant and more open to the Word, at that moment the swordsmen and axmen are activated and sent in. Update your warriors on the progress of the war. Encourage them not to grow weary.

_____ Attend to the wounded. They must be cared for by spiritual medics (those with the gifts of healing, serving, mercy, and exhortation).

_____ Have reserves to back up those who are wounded in the attack. Your alternate warriors from the original warrior prospect list can serve this function.

Enslavement

In siege warfare the battle is not over when the strongholds are pulled down. Imaginations, thoughts, and every high thing that has exalted itself above Christ still need to be enslaved. The entire thinking process must be brought into captivity, *aaichmalotizo*. This means to make one a prisoner of war, bring them into subjection, and to lead away captive by the force of a spear. Hence, when there has been a successful breach in the wall of a stronghold by the battering ram or the crow, and the defenders at the top have sufficiently defeated the enemy, this enables ground swordsmen and ax warriors to go in to fight.

A breach in a spiritual stronghold in the targeted family is indicated where you see less resistance, more openness to Christ, and more receptivity to the gospel message. Then it is time for those who use the sword and ax to go through the opening. Those skilled at using the Word and exercising the authority of God's power in deliverance are now activated. They slip through the breach and do hand-to-hand battle with the resistant thoughts. The swordsmen and axmen start with the parents and then deal with the children. They are to target the thoughts of the African-American family in question. You will know that captivity has occurred when family members "surrender" to the Lordship of Christ. When a soldier knows he's outmanned and outgunned he often will surrender, as the Iranian soldiers did in Desert Storm. Many of them gladly surrendered. When family members begin to surrender to the Lord voluntarily or are just overwhelmed by the Word of God presented to them and are thus captivated, they must be called to salvation on the spot.

Once their thoughts are captured, they must be led away. This means that someone must lead them and take them to a new place. They cannot be left to themselves. There must be immediate follow-up. Provisions have to be in place for discipleship and reprogramming of their thoughts through church, Bible study, or home study meetings. It is mandatory that ongoing, consistent checkups and accountability must occur. There should be no letup on them, so that their thoughts are constantly focused on Christ. Every opportunity must be made to expose their thoughts to the Word.

Special emphasis should be placed on obedience to Christ. This means teaching them what obedience is, how one is to obey, and why one obeys. They must be thoroughly trained in submission to the Lordship of Christ. Restrictions and limitations should be placed on what they expose themselves and their thoughts to. Every idea that is out of sync with Christ must be lovingly, biblically, and patiently challenged, until every thought is captive to the obedience of Christ.

Even when the church has successfully won battles against spiritual strongholds, they have lost ground because they forgot to take prisoners. It is the thoughts that must be made prisoners, not the people. We are not talking about restrictive rules or legalism nor referring to "do's and don'ts." That's Pharisaism. What we mean by "bringing thoughts into captivity" is the thorough, immediate, and consistent retraining of the thought processes of family members. Their minds must become enslaved to the Lordship of Christ, not to a pastor, a church, or denomination.

Evil imaginations must be destroyed, and these two Scripture passages tell us why. Among the abominable things listed in Proverbs is a "heart that deviseth wicked imaginations" (6:17–18). "Because when they knew and recognized Him as God, they did not honor and glorify him as God, or give Him thanks. But instead they became futile and godless in their thinking—with vain imaginings, foolish reasonings and stupid speculations—and their senseless minds were darkened" (Romans 1:21 AMPLIFIED).

This kind of thinking is wicked. ("Wicked" in the Hebrew is *aven*, meaning full of iniquity and mischief, unrighteous, naughty, evil.) It is also vain. ("Vain" in the Greek means following foolish and bad courses, destitute of real wisdom, perverse in actions, off the right path, idolatrous, void of result, and worthless.) These anti-Christ arguments and unrighteous rationales become spiritually resistant defenses—strongholds—and must be destroyed. Moreover, those unrighteous reckonings, perverse idolatrous reasonings, and non-Christian reflections of the mind which are void of godly wisdom must also be brought down by the force of violent of spiritual warfare.

When we find such arguments and reasonings in members of our family, it indicates the need for spiritual battle. This sort of ungodly logic and these worldly conclusions must be destroyed, and the negative thoughts must be taken captive. After the destruction of fleshly justifications, anti-Christ thoughts must then be brought into captivity. That word means to subdue, to bring into submission, and subjection. To be a prisoner is to lose one's freedom. A captive person has limits imposed on his or her activity and movement and is confined to a certain area. Therefore, those who go through the process of having strongholds destroyed in their lives must afterwards have their thoughts become POWs (Prisoners of War) to the obedience of Christ. The individual must get rid of the fleshly arguments. Then, their reasoning has to be kept perpetually in subjection and confinement.

Post-Victory Celebration

Plan a victory celebration and invite all of your warriors to come, along with the families who were delivered from the strongholds. Time should be allowed for family members to testify. All of the soldiers present should be acknowledged.

Special awards should be given out in the form of certificates of appreciation. For example: medal of valor for warriors who showed the most bravery in battle; medal of proficiency for soldiers who showed the greatest skill in the use of their weapon; medal of continuance for soldiers who were the most consistent in battle; and the medal of exuberance for soldiers who were the most powerful.

For your long-distance warriors who cannot attend, certificates can be sent by mail. In some cases, have your long-distance warriors make a videotape or send pictures of themselves. These can be shown at the celebration. If they send a tape, have them greet the group and also give the delivered family a word of encouragement. This kind of celebration is the finishing touch to a truly victorious battle.

Checklist for Encirclement, Development, Engagement, and Enslavement

_____ Are the leaders of the out-of-town groups as well as the individual archers strategically located in every direction (south, north, east, and west)? Are all active?

_____ If a group is not functioning, have you encouraged their participation or tried to find someone else to fill the gap?

_____ Is everyone aware that the signal to begin has been given?

_____ Are the medium-range warriors making full use of the name of the Lord Jesus Christ? Encourage them to pray in His name, to praise and glorify His name, and do everything in His name.

_____ Are you utilizing your newsletter as a source of encouragement to your soldiers? Do you print testimonial excerpts by persons who are achieving victory?

_____ Are you repairing or removing the wounded and replacing them with alternate soldiers?

_____ Are your team members supplied with plenty of spiritual rest, food, and water?

_____ Are you aware of any attempts by the enemy to plant spies or false soldiers, to create divisions, or any sabotage efforts from within? Are you dealing with these situations?

_____ Is everyone staying at their assigned task until a breach in the wall of the stronghold is made?

_____ Have the family members who have received Christ been followed up? Have they been put on a steady diet of God's Word?

_____ Is a discipleship program in place, with emphasis on the Lordship of Christ, submission to divine authority, and obedience?

_____ Are the people in the family being called and checked on regularly? This is very crucial.

Conclusion

This book demonstrates that many family problems exist in the African-American community. Regardless of other explanations, these problems are often the result of spiritual strongholds, resistant arguments and ideas that are contrary to the knowledge of Jesus Christ. The strongholds must be brought down, the walls must be destroyed, the ruling king and every thought brought into captivity to the obedience of Christ. To this end spiritual warfare must be waged, using the weapons of our warfare. Such a war requires an army of dedicated and spiritually gifted warriors, possessing both skill and character. They must work in unity to engage the enemy.

We must, however, avoid the trap of judging victory numerically. Sometimes with all of our manpower, planning, tedious fighting, and money spent, the result may be that only one family or one family member is delivered. "Broad is the way, that leadeth to destruction, and many there be which go in thereat.... Narrow is the way, which leadeth unto life, and few there be that find it" (Matthew 7:13–14). With all of our weapons, warfare, and commitment, still the vast majority of African-American families may not be saved. Therefore, we must by God's help try to save as many as we can as quickly as we can.

It is time for true African-American Christians to join the spiritual war to free black families. We need to take back what the enemy has taken from us as a people. We must fight with our spiritual weapons according to a spiritual strategy. We must break down the walls of Jericho; for behind those high walls await families desirous of deliverance.

Appendices

Tools
for Waging Warfare

Family Assessment Sheet

(This form is to be completed after reading the book *Breaking Strongholds in the African-American Family* and observing family interaction. Like all the forms in this appendix, it may be photocopied for multiple use.)

1. Name of Family _____

2. Address _____

3. Phone _____

4. Father/Husband's Name _____
   a. Jericho stronghold _____
   b. Stronghold arguments _____
   c. Foundation _____
   d. Related behaviors and problems _____
   e. Ruling principalities _____

5. Mother/Wife's Name_____
   a. Jericho stronghold _____
   b. Stronghold arguments _____
   c. Foundation _____
   d. Related behaviors and problems _____
   e. Ruling principalities _____

6. Children

   Name _____
   a. Jericho stronghold _____
   b. Stronghold arguments _____
   c. Foundation _____
   d. Related behaviors and problems _____
   e. Ruling principalities _____

   Name _____
   a. Jericho stronghold _____
   b. Stronghold arguments _____
   c. Foundation _____
   d. Related behaviors and problems _____
   e. Ruling principalities _____

Warrior Prospect Sheet

Long Distance (Out of Town)
Catapult Team (Praise, Prayer and Worship Group)
Focus on name of group leaders

First Choice

Name of Group Leader	Address	Phone

Second Choice (Alternate)

Warrior Prospect Sheet

Long Distance (Out of Town)
Ballista Team (Prayer Groups)
Focus on name of group leader

First Choice

Name of Group Leader	Address	Phone

Second Choice (Alternate)

Warrior Prospect Sheet

Medium Range (Same City or Neighborhood)
Tower Archers (Individual Prayer Warriors)

First Choice

Name	Address	Phone

Second Choice (Alternate)

Warrior Prospect Sheet

Medium Range (Same City and Neighborhood)
Battering Ram Team (Primary Intercessory Prayer Group)

First Choice

Name	Address	Phone

Second Choice (Alternate)

Name	Address	Phone

Warrior Prospect Sheet

Medium Range (Same City or Neighborhood)
Crow Team (Supplicating Prayer Group)

First Choice

Name	Address	Phone

Second Choice (Alternate)

Warrior Prospect Sheet

Close Range
Swordsmen (Skilled Presenters and Speakers of the Word)

First Choice

Name	Address	Phone

Second Choice (Alternate)

Warrior Prospect Sheet

Close Range
Axmen (Skilled Exercisers of the Power and Authority of God in Spiritual Warfare)

First Choice

Name	Address	Phone

Second Choice (Alternate)

Name	Address	Phone

Sample Prospect Letter

(Individual Family Approach)

Dear

    We are writing to request your participation in an exciting and critical project to deliver African-American families from spiritual bondage and see them come to know Jesus Christ as Lord and Savior. As you know, the African-American family is in crisis, with many female-headed homes, neglected children, the increasing divorce rates, as well as the expanding crisis of marital infidelity. What is needed is an army of committed, born-again Christians from the African-American community who will participate in a plan of spiritual warfare to bring down the strongholds in our families.

    Such a plan is detailed in the book *Breaking Strongholds in the African-American Family: A Practical Guide to Spiritual Warfare.* We are now implementing the plan with our family. As a relative or close friend, I have selected you as a prospective warrior to help us bring down the walls of bondage in our family. We ask you to respond in the following manner:

1. Please read the included job description sheet and related information.

2. Please pick up a copy of *Breaking Strongholds in the African-American Family* by Dr. Clarence Walker. You can purchase a copy through any local Christian bookstore. If they don't have it in stock, most will order it for you. (Or one is enclosed or one will be available for you at the first warrior meeting.)

3. Request that the bookstore call Zondervan Publishing House and order several copies.

4. Please read the book thoroughly.

5. Please prayerfully consider participating with us.

6. Fill out the reply form and mail it back to me by (specify a date).

7. Prayerfully consider a special offering to our spiritual warfare chest. I will be in touch with you by phone to further explain in more detail the various aspects of our spiritual warfare efforts. If you have any questions before that time, please contact me at the following number(s).

Your fellow soldier in Christ,

Sample Reply Letter

☐ Yes, I will participate as one of the warriors in the battle to save African-American families.

☐ I will not be able to participate directly; however, I will contribute to your spiritual warfare chest.

☐ I will not be able to participate in or support this effort at this time.

Please return to:

Coordination Captain's name
Address-Street number
City-State-Zip

115

Covenant of Participation

(Sample Covenant to be mailed to prospects)

I, [your name], having read the book *Breaking Strongholds in the African-American Family* and other information, and having prayerfully sought the Lord's direction in this matter, and having discussed this issue with the coordinating captain(s), do hereby covenant before God and with (Coordinating Captain's name) to participate in this spiritual warfare strategy as a (Warrior title), and to fulfill my duties as described in the book and outlined in my job description sheet.

Furthermore, I covenant to maintain confidentiality regarding the names and personal information given me regarding the targeted family. I will be able to commit _____ hours to this endeavor on a _____ basis.

Name (print) _____ Date _____

Signature_____

Warrior Job Description

Title: Coordinating Captain
Scope: The long-distance, medium-range, and close-range war efforts to deliver a family from strongholds.
Purpose: To coordinate the various aspects of the spiritual warfare efforts.

Duties and Responsibilities

1. To thoroughly read the book *Breaking Strongholds in the African-American Family.*

2. To recruit friends and family to be catapult and ballista team leaders, long-distance archers, tower archers, battering ram/crow team members, swordsmen, and axmen.

3. To orient the above warriors to the warfare strategy.

4. To select a targeted family.

5. To spy out and gather information for a spiritual warfare action plan.

6. To develop the spiritual warfare action plan.

7. To see that all warriors and key leaders are supplied with copies of the book and to motivate them to thoroughly read it.

8. To develop and distribute a newsletter to all warriors.

9. To give the signal to commence battle to all warriors.

10. To be an active member of the battering-ram team.

11. To stay in touch with key groups and their leaders.

12. To plan and implement the pre-victory rally and post-victory celebration.

13. To make sure all key warriors and leaders functions according to plan.

14. To mail important information and correspondence and to follow up with phone calls.

15. To secure covenants of participation.

16. To perform any additional tasks which might enhance the success of the endeavor.

17. To covenant confidentiality regarding the targeted family.

18. To work closely with the battering-ram team, crow team, swordsmen, and axmen.

19. To report to the pastor if he has given sanction or your church is participating in warfare strategy.

20. To receive reports from the catapult and ballista leaders, long-distance archers, tower archers, axmen, and swordsmen.

Warrior Job Description

Title: Catapult Team Leader
Scope: Long Distance (out of town praise and prayer coverage)
Purpose: To provide leadership to a prayer and praise group who will be providing coverage for the main intercessory and supplicatory groups, as well as those who will be sharing the Word with the family.

Name of Group _____

Duties and Responsibilities

1. To thoroughly read the book *Breaking Strongholds in the African-American Family*.

2. To recruit and/or orient members of the group to the praise and prayer strategy and to provide them with job descriptions.

3. To see that each member of my group is provided with a copy of the book and to encourage them to read it thoroughly.

4. To coordinate the prayer and praise efforts of my group to provide prayer coverage for the main intercessory and supplicatory groups, as well as those who will be sharing the Word.

5. To make sure my group meets on a regular basis for prayer and praise.

6. To engage in praise worship and prayer, targeting the evil spirits that rule the family strongholds.

7. To praise God for the salvation and deliverance of the targeted family.

8. To covenant confidentiality regarding the targeted family.

9. To read the warrior's newsletter faithfully.

10. To report to the coordinating captains.

11. To directly oversee members of prayer and praise group.

Warrior Job Description

Title: Catapult Team Member
Scope: Long Distance (out of town praise and prayer coverage)
Purpose: To provide praise and prayer coverage for the main intercessory and supplicatory groups as well as those who will be sharing the Word with the targeted family.

Duties and Responsibilities

1. To thoroughly read the book *Breaking Strongholds in the African-American Family.*

2. To be an active participant in a praise and prayer group.

3. To praise God consistently for the salvation and deliverance of the targeted family.

4. To covenant confidentiality regarding the targeted family.

5. To read the warrior's newsletter faithfully.

6. To report to the catapult team leader.

Warrior Job Description

Title: Ballista Team Leader (out of town prayer group leader)
Scope: Long Distance (Out of town prayer coverage)
Purpose: To provide leadership to a prayer group who will provide coverage for the main intercessory and supplicatory groups, as well as to those who will be sharing the Word with the family.

Name of Group _____

Duties and Responsibilities

1. To thoroughly read the book *Breaking Strongholds in the African-American Family.*

2. To recruit and/or orient my group members to the prayer strategy and provide them with job descriptions.

3. To see that each members of my group is provided with a copy of the book and to encourage them to read it thoroughly.

4. To coordinate the prayer efforts of my group to provide prayer coverage for the main intercessory and supplicatory groups as well as those who will be sharing the Word.

5. To make sure my group meets on a regular basis for prayer.

6. To engage in prayer, targeting the evil spirits that rule the family stronghold.

7. To covenant that no information regarding the targeted family will be disclosed.

8. To read the warrior's newsletter faithfully.

9. To report to the coordinating captain(s).

10. To oversee the members of my prayer group.

Warrior Job Description

Title: Archer (individual prayer warrior)
Scope: Long Distance (out of town prayer coverage)
Purpose: To provide individual prayer coverage for the main intercessory and supplicatory prayer groups, as well as those who will share the Word with the family.

Duties and Responsibilities

1. To thoroughly read the book *Breaking Strongholds in the African-American Family.*

2. To pray consistently for the two major prayer groups and those who will be sharing the Word with the targeted family.

3. To pray against the evil spirits who rule the family strongholds.

4. To pray for the salvation and deliverance of the targeted family specifically calling out their names.

5. To covenant that no information concerning the targeted family will be disclosed.

6. To stay in touch with and report to the coordinating captain.

Warrior Job Description

Title: Archer (individual prayer warrior)
Scope: Long Distance (out of town prayer coverage)
Purpose: To provide individual prayer coverage for the main intercessory and supplicatory prayer groups, as well as those who will share the Word with the family.

Duties and Responsibilities

1. To thoroughly read the book *Breaking Strongholds in the African-American Family.*

2. To pray consistently for the two major prayer groups and those who will be sharing the Word with the targeted family.

3. To pray against the evil spirits who rule the family strongholds.

4. To pray for the salvation and deliverance of the targeted family specifically calling out their names.

5. To covenant that no information concerning the targeted family will be disclosed.

6. To stay in touch with and report to the coordinating captain.

Warrior Job Description

Title: Battering Ram Team Leader
Scope: Medium Range Intercessory Prayer (in the same neighborhood)
Purpose: To be the main intercessory prayer group striving to break down the walls of the family stronghold.

Duties and Responsibilities

1. To thoroughly read the book *Breaking Strongholds in the African-American Family*.

2. To be an active participant in my prayer group.

3. To pray consistently for God to destroy the resistant arguments of the targeted family.

4. To covenant confidentiality regarding the targeted family.

5. To read the warrior's newsletter faithfully.

6. To report to coordinating captain(s).

Warrior Job Description

Title: Crow Team Member
Scope: Medium Range (supplication prayer in the same neighborhood)
Purpose: To be the main supplication group striving to pull down the walls of the family stronghold.

Duties and Responsibilities

1. To thoroughly read the book *Breaking Strongholds in the African-American Family.*

2. To be a consistent and active member in my prayer group.

3. To pray consistently for walls to come down and evil spirits which keep the family bound to be bound to themselves.

4. To covenant confidentiality regarding the targeted family.

5. To read the warrior's newsletter faithfully.

6. To report to the coordinating captain(s).

Warrior Job Description

Title: Tower Archer
Scope: Medium Range (intercessory prayer coverage for those who will be sharing the word)
Purpose: To engage in direct prayer assault against the evil spirits ruling the stronghold.

Duties and Responsibilities

1. To thoroughly read the book *Breaking Strongholds in the African-American Family.*

2. To pray consistently against the evil spirits which rule the strongholds.

3. To pray for the salvation and deliverance of the targeted family.

4. To covenant confidentiality regarding the targeted family.

5. To read the warrior's newsletter faithfully.

6. To report to the coordinating captain(s).

Warrior Job Description

Title: Swordsman
Scope: Close Range (direct contact with the family)
Purpose: To present the Word directly to the family members.

Duties and Responsibilities

1. To thoroughly read the book *Breaking Strongholds in the African-American Family*.

2. To be prepared to present the Word of God in the form of an evangelistic message to the targeted family.

3. To schedule home meetings suitable to the family's schedule to bring the gospel message.

4. To take the family through the steps of salvation.

5. To be prepared to answer questions, defend the biblical faith, and to counter the arguments of the targeted family members.

6. To follow up with the family and see that they join a discipleship program at a local church.

7. To covenant confidentiality regarding the targeted family.

8. To read the warrior's newsletter faithfully.

9. To be an active member of either a battering ram or crow team.

10. To report to the coordinating captain(s).

Warrior Job Description

Title: Axman
Scope: Close Range (direct contact with the family)
Purpose: To exercise spiritual authority and deal with spiritual bondage.

Duties and Responsibilities

1. To thoroughly read the book *Breaking Strongholds in the African-American Family*.

2. To be prepared to handle any special situations involving resistant spiritual bondage.

3. To pray with the family in their home.

4. To schedule home meetings which accommodate the family's schedule.

5. To work with swordsmen whenever necessary.

6. To be an active leader of a battering ram or crow team.

7. To covenant confidentiality regarding the targeted family.

8. To read the warrior's newsletter faithfully.

9. To report to the coordinating captain(s).

War Action Plan

(Sample workshop to use for planning stages of the war.)

Siege Element	Primary Goals	Names of Warriors	Time to Begin
Assessment			
Arrangement			
Advancement			
Encirclement			
Development			
Engagement			
Enslavement			

Special Consideration for Churches and Pastors

Churches should consider modifying the warfare plan to accommodate the needs of their congregation. Some matters to consider in modifying the plan are the following:

- Doctrinal Belief About Spiritual Gifts: This matter should be handled within the theological teaching of your church and denomination.
- Racial Make-up of Your Congregation: If your church is integrated, then you may want to broaden this program to include all families with just a slight emphasis on the African-American families.
- General Calendar and Mission of the Church: The warfare strategy can and should be adopted to themes already built within your church agenda. It can be utilized as part of your annual revivals, Black History Month, family emphasis months, prayer conferences, prayer emphasis months, and spiritual warfare emphasis events.
- General Understanding of Spiritual Warfare: Pastors may have to do a teaching series on spiritual warfare prior to trying to implement this plan. The more your people understand spiritual warfare the more they will be willing to get involved in it. You should probably use this book as the basis of your teaching.
- General Support of Both Leadership and Congregation: How much backing the pastors receive from the church leadership is critical to how well a church utilizes this plan. In traditional churches that have older leaders

who have been at the church for a number of years, there may be resistance to such a plan. Moreover, pastors need to consider the numbers and spiritual maturity of their leadership in determining how to modify the plan to the needs of their church.

- The Quality of Your Relationship as a Church to Others Outside of Your Area: Since the plan calls for recruiting warriors from a distance this requires having a network relationship with churches outside of your area. Thus, the more isolated a church is, the more difficult they may find it to implement this plan.

- The Quality of the Organization and Systems of Your Church: The more organized and systematized your church is, the more you will be able to implement this agenda. The nature of the structure of your church and how it functions should be considered in your modifying of this plan.

Appendix 3

Special Consideration for Individual Family Approaches

- Personal Doctrinal Beliefs Regarding Spiritual Gifts: It is recommended that this matter be dealt with according to your personal doctrine as related to your church and denomination.
- General Support of Pastor and Church: As an individual you should be an active member of some Bible believing and preaching church. Remember that "we wrestle." Your church is the most logical place to secure the army you will need to address the family strongholds. You should first seek the approval and sanction of your pastor. If he or she is not familiar with this book introduce it to them. If the plan can be worked through your local church that is how it should be implemented. If you're a member of a church that does not support your effort and you decide to implement the program on your own, then it is recommended that you focus on your family, either nuclear or extended. Inform your pastor what you will be doing by letter and follow up by phone. Let them know that you are not trying to be rebellious against their leadership, but the salvation of your family is important to you and that it is necessary to proceed with the plan.

  Sometimes the pastor may indicate that he wants you to wait. You should submit to this counsel, however, and obtain a set time from him when you can start. Get as specific a date as you can. When that time comes you should inform the pastor by letter of the fact that the deadline for beginning has come. Request a meeting with him to go over the plan. During this time that you are waiting you may want to provide your pastor with a copy of the book so he can read it for himself.

- Quality of Your Personal Relationship with Others Outside Your Area: Since the plan calls for an army of people including people who live outside your neighborhood and beyond, how well you have established and are able to utilize these friends and family becomes critical to the success of the plan.
- Quality of Your Skills As an Organizer and an Administrator: To implement the warfare strategy in this book requires someone with exceptional organizational and administrative abilities. The better one's skills are, the more likely their chance to succeed. Sometimes it may require recruiting someone to co-partner with you who has the skills you lack. In some cases it may mean you taking a step back allowing someone else to actually function as organizer of the plan. Job description sheets, clear boundaries of function, and clear lines of authority will become important to avoid potential strife or rivalry.
- Number of Persons Involved: One of the challenges you will face as an individual is how many actual friends and family you will be able to recruit. Numbers can be a problem either way—that is, you can have too few involved or too many. One must prayerfully address the issue of numbers.

Sample Letter

Sample Letter

(This letter is to be used by participating churches. It may be reproduced as desired.)

Dear Member (or member's name):

We are writing to request your participation in an exciting and critical church project to deliver African-American families from spiritual bondage and to see that they come to know Jesus Christ as Lord and Savior. As you know the African-American family is in a crisis, with growing female-headed, single-parent homes, the growing number of abused and neglected children, the increasing divorce rate, as well as the expanding crisis of marital infidelity. What is needed is an army of committed, born-again Christians from the African-American Christian community who will participate in a plan of spiritual warfare to bring down the strongholds in our families. Such a plan is available through the book *Breaking Strongholds in the African-American Family*. There are several families in our congregation and in the neighborhood surrounding our church who are in bondage to spiritual strongholds. As your pastor, I am calling the church to a time of spiritual warfare. You will receive more information about this endeavor in the coming weeks. _____ will serve as our church coordinating captain for this endeavor. Those of you who decide to participate will be contacted by the captain as to specific details of our plan and your specific role. Meanwhile we are requesting that you abide by the following:

1. Please secure a copy of the book *Breaking Strongholds in the African-American Family* by Dr. Clarence Walker and read it thoroughly. The book(s) can be secured from our church by contacting _____. The cost is $9.99.
2. Please prayerfully consider participating in this project with us.
3. Prayerfully consider giving a sacrificial offering to our "Spiritual Warfare Chest" to financially support this effort.
4. Pray for this project daily.

We are looking forward to great victory in the battle to save families and hope that you are one of the warriors who will share in the triumph.

Yours in Christ,

(Pastor's name)

Bibliography

Butler, Trent C. *Holman Bible Dictionary*. Nashville: Holman Bible Publishers, 1991.

Chancellor, Williams. *The Destruction of Black Civilization*. Chicago: Third World Press, 1974.

Clarke, John Henrik, and J. A. Rogers. *World's Great Men of Color*. Vol. 2. Edited by J. A. Rogers. New York: Collier Books/Macmillan, 1972.

Diop, Cheikh Anita. *The African Origin of Civilization: Myth or Reality*. New York: Lawrence Hill, 1974.

Douglas, J. D. *New Commentary on the Whole Bible*. Wheaton, Ill.: Tyndale House, 1990.

Earle, Ralph. *Word Meanings in the New Testament*. Grand Rapids: Baker Book House, 1986.

Freeman, James. *Manners and Customs of the Bible*. South Plainfield, N.J.: Logos International, 1977.

Grier, William, and Rice Cobbs. *Black Rage*. New York: Basic Books, 1968.

Hare, Nathan, and Julia Hare. *The Endangered Black Family: Coping with the Unisexualization and Coming Extension of the Black Race*. San Francisco: Black Think Tank, 1984.

Johnson, John L. *The Black Biblical Heritage*. Nashville: Winston-Derek Publishers, 1991.

Kunjufu, J. *Countering the Conspiracy to Destroy Black Boys*. Chicago: Afro-Am Publishing, 1984.

Martin, Elmer, and Joanne Mitchell Martin. *The Black Extended Family*. Chicago: University of Chicago Press, 1978.

McCray, Walter. *The Black Presence in the Bible*. Chicago: Black Light Fellowship, 1990.

McKissic, William Dwight. *Beyond Roots: In Search of Blacks in the Bible*. Wenonah, N.J.: Renaissance Productions, 1990.

Packer, J. I., Merrill C. Tenney, and William White, Jr., eds. *The Bible Almanac*. Nashville: Thomas Nelson, 1980.

Poissant, Alvin. *Why Blacks Kill Blacks*. New York: Emerson Hall, 1972.

Richards, Lawrence O. *Revell Bible Dictionary*. Old Tappan, N.J.: Fleming H. Revell, 1990.

Russell, Gedder Groset. *Webster's New Dictionary*. New York: Windsor Court, 1990.

Smith, William. *Smith's Bible Dictionary*. Reprint, Nashville: Thomas Nelson, 1986.

Staples, Robert. *Black Masculinity: The Black Male's Role in American Society*. Oakland, Calif.: Black Scholar Press, 1982.

Stone, Merlin. *When God Was a Woman*. New York: Harcourt Brace, 1976.

Unger, Merrill F. *Unger's Bible Dictionary*. Chicago: Moody Press, 1957.

Vine, W. E., Merrill F. Unger, and William White, Jr. *Complete Expository Dictionary of Old and New Testament Words*. Nashville: Thomas Nelson, 1985.

Webster New Collegiate Dictionary. Springfield, Mass.: Merriam-Webster, 1975.

Wuest, David. *Word Studies in the Greek New Testament*. Vol. 2. Grand Rapids: William B. Eerdmans, 1973.

Zodhiates, Spiros. *The Complete Word Study Dictionary: New Testament*. Iowa Falls, Iowa: World Bible Publishers, 1992.

Notes

Chapter One

1. Lawrence O. Richards, *Revell Bible Dictionary* (Old Tappan, N.J.: Revell, 1990), 1010.

Chapter Two

1. William H. Grier and Price M. Cobbs, *Black Rage* (New York: Basic Books, 1968), 20–30.
2. *Webster's New Collegiate Dictionary* (Springfield, Mass.: Merriam, 1990), 53.
3. W. E. Vine, Merrill F. Unger, William White, Jr., eds. *Vine's Complete Expository Dictionary of Old Testament Words* (Nashville: Thomas Nelson, 1968), 26.
4. Ibid.
5. Elmer P. Martin and Joanne Mitchell-Martin, *The Black Extended Family* (Chicago: University of Chicago Press, 1978), 95.
6. William Chancellor, *The Destruction of Black Civilization* (Chicago: University of Chicago Press, 1978), 95.
7. Ibid., 231.
8. Merlin Stone, *When God Was a Woman* (New York: Harcourt Brace, 1976), 163–80.

Chapter Three

1. Alvin Poissant, *Why Blacks Kill Blacks* (New York: Emerson Hall, 1972), 59–80.
2. William Dwight McKissic, *Beyond Roots: In Search of Blacks in the Bible* (Wenonah, N.J.: Renaissance Productions, 1990), 20.
3. J. D. Douglas, ed., *New Commentary on the Whole Bible Old Testament* (Wheaton, Ill.: Tyndale House, 1990), 22.
4. J. I. Packer, Merrill C. Tenney, William White Jr., eds., *The Bible Almanac* (Nashville: Thomas Nelson, 1980), 130–31.
5. W. E. Vine, Merrill F. Unger, William White, Jr., eds. *Vine's Complete Expository Dictionary of Old Testament Words* (Nashville: Thomas Nelson, 1985), 110.
6. Robert Staples, *Black Muscularity: The Black Male's Role in American Society* (Oakland, Calif.: Black Scholar Press, 1982.

Chapter Four

1. William Dwight McKissic, *Beyond Roots: In Search of Blacks in the Bible* (Wenonah, N.J.: Renaissance Productions, 1990), 22.
2. Ibid.
3. Ibid.
4. J. A. Rogers, ed. *World's Great Men of Color*, vol. 2 (New York: Collier Books/Macmillan, 1972).
5. John L. Johnson, *The Black Biblical Heritage* (Nashville: Winston-Derek, 1991), 145.
6. Merlin Stone, *When God Was a Woman* (New York: Harcourt Brace, 1976), 173–75.

Chapter Five

1. J. Kunjufu, *Countering the Conspiracy to Destroy Black Boys* (Chicago: Afro-Am Publishing, 1984).
2. Alvin Poissant, *Why Blacks Kill Blacks* (New York: Emerson Hall, 1972), 59–80.

Chapter Six

1. Merrill F. Unger, *Unger's Bible Dictionary* (Chicago: Moody Press, 1957), 89.
2. Spiros Zodhiates, *The Complete Word Study Dictionary: New Testament* (Iowa Falls, Iowa: World Bible Publishers, 1992), 699.
3. Unger, *Unger's Bible Dictionary*, 91.
4. William Smith, *Smith's Bible Dictionary* (Reprint, Nashville: Thomas Nelson, 1986), 736.
5. Unger, *Unger's Bible Dictionary*, 89–95.
6. David Wuest, *Word Studies in the Greek New Testament*, vol. 2 (Grand Rapids: Eerdmans, 1973), 143.
7. Ibid., 144.
8. Unger, *Unger's Bible Dictionary*, 91.
9. J. I. Packer, Merrill C. Tenney, William White Jr., eds., *The Bible Almanac* (Nashville: Thomas Nelson, 1980), 309.
10. W. E. Vine, Merrill F. Unger, William White, Jr., eds. *Vine's Complete Expository Dictionary of Old and New Testament Words* (Nashville: Thomas Nelson, 1985), 164.

11. James W. Freeman, *Manners and Customs of the Bible* (South Plainfield, N.J.: Logos International, 1972), 295.

12. Trent C. Butler, *Holman's Bible Dictionary* (Nashville: Holman Bible Publishers, 1991), 101–2.

13. Packer et al., *The Bible Almanac*, 309.

14. Ibid., 351.

Chapter Eight

1. Ralph Earle, *Word Meanings in the New Testament* (Grand Rapids: Baker, 1986), 356.

2. William Smith, *Smith's Bible Dictionary* (Reprint, Nashville: Thomas Nelson, 1986), 737.

3. Ibid., 736.